Writing Program Administration

Journal of the
Council of Writing Program Administrators

Editor
Lori Ostergaard .... Oakland University

Associate Editors
Jacob Babb .... Indiana University Southeast
Jim Nugent .... Oakland University

Assistant Editors
Katie McWain .... University of Nebraska–Lincoln
Molly E. Ubbesen .... University of Wisconsin–Milwaukee

Book Review Editor
Courtney Adams Wooten .... Stephen F. Austin State University

Ads Manager
Amy Cicchino .... Florida State University

Editorial Board
Bradley Bleck .... Spokane Falls Community College
Micheal Callaway .... Mesa Community College
Casie Fedukovich .... North Carolina State University
Tarez Samra Graban .... Florida State University
Asao B. Inoue .... University of Washington Tacoma
Seth Kahn .... West Chester University
Carrie Leverenz .... Texas Christian University
Mandy Macklin .... University of Washington
Mark McBeth .... John Jay College of Criminal Justice/CUNY
Laura Micciche .... University of Cincinnati
Charles Paine .... University of New Mexico
E. Shelley Reid .... George Mason University
Rochelle (Shelley) Rodrigo .... University of Arizona
Ellen Schendel .... Grand Valley State University
Virginia Schwarz .... University of Wisconsin–Madison
Wendy Sharer .... East Carolina University
Amy Ferdinandt Stolley .... Grand Valley State University
Elizabeth Vander Lei .... Calvin College
Scott Warnock .... Drexel University

WPA: Writing Program Administration (ISSN: 0196-4682) is published twice per year—fall and spring—by the Council of Writing Program Administrators. Production and printing of *WPA: Writing Program Administration* is managed by Parlor Press.

Council of Writing Program Administrators

Executive Board

The Council of Writing Program Administrators is a national association of college and university faculty who serve or have served as directors of first-year composition or writing programs, coordinators of writing centers and writing workshops, chairpersons and members of writing-program-related committees, or in similar administrative capacities. The Council of Writing Program Administrators is an affiliate of the Association of American Colleges and the Modern Language Association.

Dominic DelliCarpini, President .... York College of Pennsylvania
Mark Blaauw-Hara, Vice President .... North Central Michigan College
Susan Miller-Cochran, Immediate Past President .... University of Arizona
Asao Inoue .... University of Washington Tacoma
Karen Keaton Jackson .... North Carolina Central University
Cheri Lemieux Spiegel .... Northern Virginia Community College
Cristyn Elder .... University of New Mexico
Paula Patch .... Elon University
Scott Warnock .... Drexel University
Sheila Carter-Tod .... Virginia Tech
Genevieve Garcia de Mueller .... University of Texas Rio Grande Valley
Staci Perryman-Clark .... Western Michigan University

Ex Officio Members

Christine Cucciarre, Treasurer .... University of Delaware
Michael McCamley, Secretary .... University of Delaware
Shirley K Rose
       Director, Consultant-Evaluator Service (CES) .... Arizona State University
Michael Pemberton, Associate Director, CES .... Georgia Southern University
Lori Ostergaard, Editor, *WPA* .... Oakland University
Jacob Babb, Associate Editor, *WPA* .... Indiana University Southeast
Jim Nugent, Associate Editor, *WPA* .... Oakland University
Virginia Schwarz, Chair, WPA-GO .... University of Wisconsin–Madison
Mandy Macklin, Vice Chair, WPA-GO .... University of Washington

Guide for Authors

WPA: Writing Program Administration publishes empirical and theoretical research on issues in writing program administration. We publish a wide range of research in various formats, research that not only helps both titled and untitled administrators of writing programs do their jobs, but also helps our discipline advance academically, institutionally, and nationally.
Possible topics of interest include:

- writing faculty professional development
- writing program creation and design
- uses for national learning outcomes and statements that impact writing programs
- classroom research studies
- labor conditions: material, practical, fiscal
- WAC/WID/WC/CAC (or other sites of communication/writing in academic settings)
- writing centers and writing center studies
- teaching writing with electronic texts (multimodality) and teaching in digital spaces
- theory, practice, and philosophy of writing program administration
- outreach and advocacy
- curriculum development
- writing program assessment
- WPA history and historical work
- national and regional trends in education and their impact on WPA work
- issues of professional advancement and writing program administration
- diversity and WPA work
- writing programs in a variety of educational locations (SLACs, HBCUs, two-year colleges, Hispanic schools, non-traditional schools, dual credit or concurrent enrollment programs, prison writing programs)
- interdisciplinary work that informs WPA practices

This list is meant to be suggestive, not exhaustive. Contributions must be appropriate to the interests and concerns of the journal and its readership. The editors welcome empirical research (quantitative as well as qualitative), historical research, and theoretical, essayistic, and practical pieces.

Submission Guidelines

Please check the *WPA* website for complete submissions guidelines and to download the required coversheet. In general, submissions should:

- be a maximum 7,500 words;
- be styled according to either the *MLA Handbook* (8th edition) or the *Publication Manual of the American Psychological Association* (6th edition), as appropriate to the nature of your research;

- include an abstract (maximum 200 words);
- contain no identifying information;
- be submitted as a .doc or .docx format file; and
- use tables, notes, figures, and appendices sparingly and judiciously.

Submissions that do not follow these guidelines or that are missing the cover page will be returned to authors before review.

Reviews

WPA:Writing Program Administration publishes both review essays of multiple books and reviews of individual books related to writing programs and their administration. If you are interested in reviewing texts or recommending books for possible review, please contact the book review editor at wpabookreviews@gmail.com.

Announcements and Calls

Relevant announcements and calls for papers may be published as space permits. Announcements should not exceed 500 words, and calls for proposals or participation should not exceed 1,000 words. Submission deadlines in calls should be no sooner than January 1 for the fall issue and June 1 for the spring issue. Please email your calls and announcements to wpaeditors@gmail.com and include the text in both the body of the message and as a .doc or .docx attachment.

Correspondence

Correspondence relating to the journal, submissions, or editorial issues should be sent to wpaeditors@gmail.com.

Subscriptions

WPA: Writing Program Administration is published twice per year—fall and spring—by the Council of Writing Program Administrators. Members of the council receive a subscription to the journal and access to the *WPA* archives as part of their membership. Join the council at http://wpacouncil.org. Information about library subscriptions is available at http://wpacouncil.org/library-memberships.

Writing Program Administration

Journal of the
Council of Writing Program Administrators
Volume 41.2 (Spring 2018)

Contents

Dancing the Same Dances: *WPA*, 1979–1981 7
   Lori Ostergaard, Jim Nugent, and Jacob Babb

Inez in Transition: Using Case Study to Explore the Experiences of
Underrepresented Students in First-Year Composition 17
   Christina Saidy

Making (Collective) Memory Public: WPA Histories in Dialogue 35
   Kelly Ritter

Adapting Writing about Writing: Curricular Implications of Cross-
Institutional Data from the Writing Transfer Project 65
   Carol Hayes, Ed Jones, Gwen Gorzelsky, and
   Dana L. Driscoll

Preparing Graduate Students for the Field: A Graduate Student Praxis
Heuristic for WPA Professionalization and Institutional Politics 89
   Ashton Foley-Schramm, Bridget Fullerton, Eileen M. James,
   and Jenna Morton-Aiken

"Everyone Should Have a Plan": A Neoliberal Primer for
Writing Program Directors 104
   Nancy Welch

Austerity and the Scales of Writing Program Administration:
Some Reflections on the 2017 CWPA Conference 113
   Tony Scott

Review Essay

Beyond Satisfaction: Assessing the Goals and Impacts of
Faculty Development 122
   E. Shelley Reid

Book Reviews

Learning on the Job and Learning from the Job: A Review of
The Working Lives of New Writing Center Directors 136
   Brandy Lyn G. Brown

Collaborating to Support Graduate Student Writers:
Working beyond Disciplinary and Institutional Silos 143
   Daveena Tauber

Announcement 149

Dancing the Same Dances: *WPA*, 1979–1981

Lori Ostergaard, Jim Nugent, and Jacob Babb

> *When I sat down to write these chapters, one of my central (if tacit) purposes was to provide a shared past, a story of ancestors. I am trying here to build a fire around which we can sit and discover that we do know the same stories, and dance the same dances.*
>
> —Robert J. Connors,
> *Composition-Rhetoric: Backgrounds, Theory, and Pedagogy* (18)

We opened our first issue as editors by looking back at the genesis of *WPA*, which was first published as a newsletter and evolved into a journal in 1979 under the editorship of Kenneth Bruffee. Here we continue our historical review and, in future issues, our editors' introductions will continue to reexamine *WPA*'s legacy of contributions to research, advocacy, and community. In tracing the history of the journal that we are now so privileged to edit, we hope to honor the legacy of those who came before us; to acknowledge the work that the council, its journal, and its members performed in nurturing our field; and to "build a fire around which we can sit" and share important stories about our community. We offer these retrospective pieces not just to highlight early works that may interest contemporary WPAs, but to also illustrate our field's connection to the issues, problems, practices, failures, and successes of the past. In each new issue, we will seek both to advance the best work of contemporary scholars, teachers, and administrators in our field and to contemplate how we fit into the legacy that began with Bruffee's editorship in 1979.

WPA's first official issue as a journal (vol. 3, no. 1) featured work from familiar scholars: Maxine Hairston, Erika Lindemann, and Greg Larkin. The issue focused "on program definition and evaluation" (8) and featured Hairston's "What Freshman Directors Need to Know about Evaluating

Writing Programs." Hariston called on "administrators at all levels to take a more professional and objective look at teaching writing than we have ever done in the past" (11), and she shared insights into program evaluation that she and James Kinneavy developed at the University of Texas at Austin. Hairston's article was six pages long and cited no external sources, but it relied heavily on her experience as a WPA. In its first three years, *WPA* published 33 articles over eight issues. Each issue was an average of 39 pages long and articles averaged about five pages each. Fewer than one in three of those articles cited outside experts or studies. Then, as now, WPAs were *the experts*, and *WPA* had provided them with a pioneering scholarly platform to share their expertise and develop their own corpus of research.

While Hairston's article demonstrated how program administrators should evaluate their own programs, Erika Lindemann's article "Evaluating Writing Programs: What an Outside Evaluator Looks For" introduced readers to the concept of external program evaluation, explained how the evaluation process works, and provided a guide for how to plan an external evaluation. We wrote to Lindemann to ask her to reflect on this article and her work with the Consultant Evaluator Program, which was announced in vol. 3, no. 2 (see figure 1). Lindemann recalls that, at the time of the first issue, there were only a small number of WPAs who regularly attended CCCC and MLA and "the role of a WPA was evolving as faculty members trained in other areas of English studies became professionally committed to teaching writing, especially in first-year writing programs." CWPA president Harvey S. Wiener first called for the creation of an external evaluator program in a 1978 issue of the *WPA Newsletter*, and Lindemann notes that it was probably Wiener who asked her to contribute this article:

> He and Ken Bruffee were hoping to turn the *WPA Newsletter* into a refereed journal, and members of the editorial board were all engaged in enlisting articles that would advance the scholarship of writing program administration. We were eager to define, for ourselves and for other colleagues in our home institutions, what writing program administration is (and could be).

Lindemann, who had been trained as a medievalist but was tapped to become an administrator "one year into [her] first full-time faculty appointment to direct the writing program at the University of South Carolina," sat on the first *WPA* editorial board. When Wiener asked her to write "Evaluating Writing Programs," she notes that she "had already been thinking about ways to improve the writing program [she had] inherited as a faculty member." At that time she had conducted two external reviews and a self-study of her program, so her article drew largely from those experiences.

While she was not identified in the 1980 *WPA* article, "Writing Program Evaluation: An Outline for Self-Study" (WPA Board), Lindemann notes that she was responsible for compiling the guidelines presented there, which were originally developed at a workshop held at the April 1980 CCCC convention in Washington, DC. The goal of the CCCC workshop, she says, "was to flesh out the four areas discussed in my 1979 essay—curriculum, program administration, teacher training/faculty development, and support services—by drafting a 'set of guidelines and standards' for writing program self-study." She remarks that participants broke into groups "charged with creating subcategories within the four broader areas and developing questions that WPAs could use as a heuristic, a tool" to review their own programs. Lindemann was chosen to record the discussions and compile each report, which she "combined, edited, and submitted" to Bruffee for publication. She notes that the guidelines, which were "sanctioned by WPA, offered significant backing not only for recommendations that consultant-evaluators felt necessary to make but also for worthy improvements that faculty members and administrators wished to implement in improving their own programs." As Lindemann's work demonstrates, the journal played a vital role in disseminating information about, and lending additional authority to, the consultant-evaluator program in the early 1980s.

WPA consultation service

WPA will offer a service of writing program consultation and evaluation beginning April, 1980.

WPA consultants will be current or former directors of writing programs in American colleges and universities who have been trained by WPA in techniques of program evaluation, curriculum development, student needs, and organizational structure.

Consultants will be available, within the limits of program funds, to visit campuses; to interview faculty, students, and administrative officers; and to prepare written reports that appraise the strengths and limitations of existing programs and suggest improvements appropriate to an institution's needs and resources.

The service is available to public and private institutions, two-year and four-year colleges, universities, and professional schools. WPA will provide a small grant, predicated on need, to institutions selected to take part in the program. The supplement is intended to defray part of the cost of the consultation visit and report.

For application forms, write to Harvey S. Wiener, President, Council of Writing Program Administrators, La Guardia College, City University of New York, 31-10 Thomson Avenue, Long Island City, New York 11101. Applications must be received by February 15, 1980.

This service of the Council of Writing Program Administrators is supported in part by a grant from the Exxon Foundation.

Figure 1. First announcement for the WPA consultation service, published in the winter 1979 issue of *WPA* (6).

Much like the authors in this issue, scholars gracing the early pages of *WPA* took on pressing problems in the field and offered practical ideas that WPAs could apply at their own institutions. For example, the fall 1980 issue of *WPA* featured an article by Robert R. Bataille, who warned that

> if we do not challenge everywhere the tendency to hire poorly qualified faculty at low rank and salary to teach composition courses, we will continue to convey the message—to our higher administration, to our colleagues, and to our constituencies outside the institution—that composition teaching and research in related fields are, media propaganda notwithstanding, still relatively unimportant to a good college education. (17)

Bataille's article, titled "Hiring Composition Specialists," provided strategies for writing job ads that would attract specialists in composition, gave advice on how to read application letters and CVs to evaluate an applicant's interest and experience in composition teaching, and discussed how to evaluate an applicant's "formal training" in the field (20). In reflecting on what that training might look like, Bataille provided what he referred to as "a slightly mad, impossibly idealistic recipe for a training program for composition specialists" that included courses in "the theory of modern rhetoric, theory of composition, classical rhetoric, the major practical approaches to composition, and perhaps modern persuasion theory" (20). He recommended courses in linguistics and teaching English as a second language, statistics and research design, teaching reading, and, because the field had begun investigating cognition,[1] Bataille recommended that "a course in cognitive psychology might also help" prepare teachers of college composition (21).

The topic of developing a graduate program was also very much in the air in the early 1980s. The same year Bataille published his "slightly mad" list of graduate courses, Richard L. Graves and Harry M. Solomon published a national survey of new composition-rhetoric graduate courses in *Freshman English News*. Graves and Solomon surveyed 89 graduate programs and found that 61 of such programs had developed one or more new graduate-level courses in composition between the years 1974 and 1979. Their survey identified six categories of graduate courses in the field: "(1) The Teaching of Rhetoric and Composition, (2) Theory of Rhetoric and Composition, (3) Advanced Writing, (4) Basic Writing, (5) Research in Rhetoric and Composition, and (6) Stylistics" (1). The following year, the *Journal of Basic Writing* dedicated their entire spring/summer issue to the topic of graduate education and professional development, featuring descriptions of doctoral programs in composition that were authored by

John Brereton (Wayne State University) and Joseph Comprone (University of Louisville), and profiles of writing instructor training programs by Richard C. Gebhardt (Findlay College) and Charles Moran (University of Massachusetts Amherst). Bataille's article on hiring composition specialists illustrated the scarcity of faculty who were expert in the teaching of writing. But that need was already being met by new graduate courses and new doctoral programs in rhetoric and composition.

While articles about graduate programs and pedagogy appeared regularly in the pages of *WPA*, the early journal also addressed issues related to assessment, professional development, and program evaluation. In keeping with its mission to address issues of urgent interest to WPAs, the winter 1980 issue featured its first forum with five articles on faculty professional development: two longer works examining "Faculty Indifference to Writing" (Marius) and "Faculty Development Through Professional Collaboration" (Lyons), and three short articles dedicated to "Helping Faculty Make Rewarding Assignments" (Nold), "Six Steps Toward Departmental Engagement in Composition" (Bonner), and "Three Kinds of Writing Workshops for English Teachers" (Brothers). This forum was taken on as a response to budget reductions and declining enrollment in English major programs, which had forced many senior English literature faculty into first-year writing classrooms. The forum sought to provide WPAs with strategies "to help these highly trained faculty, deeply committed in other areas of the profession" to fulfill their teaching responsibilities in composition (7).

In the fall of 1981, Bruffee dedicated an entire issue to labor conditions in first-year writing. Included among articles by Donald A. McQuade, Susan Blank and Beth Greenberg, Wayne C. Booth, and Geoffrey S. Weinman was a report by Ben W. McClelland describing a CWPA survey of 156 US writing programs. McClelland noted that nearly half of writing faculty at surveyed institutions were designated part-time. The survey also revealed that while 59% of these institutions required that their part-time faculty possess at least an MA, the remaining 41% required "no more than a B.A. or B.S." (13). McClelland reported on the percentage of courses taught by part-time faculty in the departments he surveyed, maximum teaching loads for part-time faculty, percentage of departments who provided benefits to their adjunct faculty, and the salary ranges for part-timers (see figure 2).

Wayne C. Booth's article in this special issue on labor was titled "A Cheap, Efficient, Challenging, Sure-Fire and Obvious Device for Combatting the Major Scandal in Higher Education Today." Booth began by decrying the uncivilized state of higher education where full-time faculty seemed content "with the persisting scandal of intellectual, economic, and social abuse of part-time faculty" (35). He enumerated those abuses—

low wages, lack of job security, lack of representation in university governance—and suggested that any institution wishing to demonstrate that it was committed to education should develop "a serious program of continuing education for all beginning faculty members, and [take] part-time teachers as seriously as lucky tenured teachers" (36).

> **Rank and salary.** Only 25 percent of the institutions reporting have academic ranks for part-time faculty and only 24 percent provide any fringe benefits to part-time faculty. The table below sets forth the data on the salary range for part-time faculty at all institutions reporting.
>
> **Salary Range Table**
>
> | Salary ranges per semester hour | Percentage of institutions reporting |
> |---|---|
> | Below $300 | 30 |
> | $300-399 | 42 |
> | $400-499 | 13 |
> | Above $500 | 15 |

Figure 2. McClelland's explanation and table demonstrating salary ranges for part-time faculty at the surveyed institutions (15).

Unlike Booth, who waxed nostalgic for his days as a new adjunct at the University of Chicago, Susan Blank and Beth Greenberg described the struggles they faced as part-time faculty in "Living at the Bottom." This article, which was reprinted from a 1977 issue of *The Radical Teacher*, demonstrated the "series of contradictions, each one prickly and confining and ultimately exploitative" that defined the authors' work as part-time instructors (9). For example, they bemoaned the union rules that were designed to prevent them from being exploited through overwork but instead kept them "underemployed by making it illegal for [them] to get enough work" to earn a living wage at only one college (9). They observed that while teaching is recognized as a profession, they were "in many ways" more like migrant workers who never knew where they would have to go next to find work (10). Their article examined the consequences of this piecemeal work, including the loneliness stemming from their inability to connect with colleagues who may be "uprooted the next term" (11), and the contradictions between their feeling "slighted when excluded from professional duties . . . [but] exploited when [they were] asked to perform these duties for no pay" (11).

In these early issues we find writing faculty and WPAs giving voice to the problems that continue to challenge our field today. The pages of this journal also document how far we have come in developing the professional apparatuses, administrative practices, and research methods that facilitate and lend credibility to our work. While *WPA* cannot provide space for the kind of "collective memory" that Kelly Ritter advocates in her article in the present issue, this journal's archives demonstrate the collective power of this organization and its members to develop an identity for program administrators and to define our field, our programs, and our pedagogy.

In This Issue

We are proud to share four articles, two plenary presentations, and three book reviews this spring. This issue is a transitional one, featuring two works—Christina Saidy's "Inez in Transition" and Kelly Ritter's "Making (Collective) Memory Public"— that the current editorial team approved for publication, and two works—Carol Hayes, Edmund Jones, Gwen Gorzelsky, and Dana L. Driscoll's "Adapting Writing about Writing," and Ashton Foley, Bridget Fullerton, Eileen James, and Jenna Morton-Aiken's "Preparing Graduate Students for the Field"—that were selected and developed by the previous editors. We're thrilled to see all of these fine works "dance the same dances" that Bruffee, Lindemann, Bataille, and others began for us nearly four decades ago. This issue also features two works from the 2017 CWPA conference in Knoxville. Nancy Welch provides us with a version of her presentation, "'Everyone Should Have a Plan': A Neoliberal Primer for Writing Program Directors," while Tony Scott offers a synthesis of some of the lessons he took away from individual sessions during the conference in "Austerity and the Scales of Writing Program Administration: Some Reflections on the 2017 CWPA Conference."

Reviews

Courtney Adams Wooten's tenure as book review editor begins with this issue, and she would like to invite those in the field who wish to write a review—whether they have a book in mind or not—to contact her at wpabookreviews@gmail.com.

This issue includes one book review essay and two individual book reviews. First, E. Shelley Reid reviews two recent books about faculty development in her review essay "Beyond Satisfaction: Assessing the Goals and Impacts of Faculty Development." Brandy Lyn G. Brown's "Learning on the Job" offers a review of the award-winning book *The Working Lives of New Writing Center Faculty* by Nicole I. Caswell, Jackie Grutsch McKinney, and Rebecca Jackson. Finally, Daveena Tauber reviews a collection about programs developed to support graduate student writers in her review, titled "Collaborating to Support Graduate Student Writers: Working beyond Disciplinary and Institutional Silos."

A New Home for the Travelogue

The *WPA* travelogue, which has traditionally appeared in the spring issue of the journal, will appear this year in a special online supplement to the journal. While Shirley Rose's interview with WPAs at the host institutions will remain the central feature of the travelogue, an online forum will allow us to offer additional information about the conference's host institutions. Look for information about the travelogue in early June on social media, the WPA-L listserv, and an email to the CWPA membership.

Acknowledgments

Finally, we would like to take a moment to thank our home institutions for their support of our work editing *WPA*. Dean Kevin Corcoran of the College of Arts and Sciences at Oakland University (OU) has provided office space, travel funds, course releases, and other resources to make the work of editing this journal considerably easier. Lori and Jim are grateful to Dean Corcoran for making a home for *WPA* at OU and for recognizing the importance of this journal to the field and to the work of our own writing program and department. Jacob is grateful for the support of Uric Dufrene, Indiana University Southeast's executive vice chancellor of academic affairs, for providing funding to ensure that Jacob can attend the CWPA Conference each summer during our editorship.

The quality of the articles published in *WPA* are owing both to the hard work of our authors and to the constructive, knowledgeable, and timely feedback provided by a small army of dedicated reviewers. We are grateful to the following reviewers for their generous and supportive responses to the submissions we have received since June 2017. Our field is better for the service of Heather Brook Adams, Susan Delaney Adams, Valerie Balester, Deb Balzhiser, Charles Bazerman, Shane Borrowman, Bob Broad, Nicole I. Caswell, Pamela Childers, Michael Day, Amy J. Devitt, Doug Downs, Heidi Estrem, Harley Ferris, Crystal N. Fodrey, Teresa Grettano, Kay Halasek, Kristine Hansen, Susanmarie Harrington, Bruce Horner, Sarah Z. Johnson, Seth Kahn, Jeffrey Klausman, Michelle LaFrance, Paula Mathieu, Randall McClure, Miles McCrimmon, Annie Mendenhall, Tracy Ann Morse, Jessica Nastal-Dema, Kat O'Meara, Mya Poe, E. Shelley Reid, Donna Strickland, and Howard Tinberg.

NOTE

1. Of course, cognitive approaches were prevalent in a number of composition journals during this time. Karl K. Taylor's *"Doors* English: The Cognitive Basis of Rhetorical Models" appeared in the spring/summer 1979 issue of the *Journal of Basic Writing*; Linda Flower's "Writer-Based Prose: A Cognitive Basis for Problems in Writing" and Andrea A. Lunsford's "Cognitive Development and the Basic Writer" were published in *College English* one year before Bataille's article; Linda Flower and John R. Hayes' article "The Cognition of Discovery: Defining a Rhetorical Problem" appeared in the February 1980 issue of *College Composition and Communication*; and Mike Rose's "Rigid Rules, Inflexible Plans, and the Stifling of Language: A Cognitivist Analysis of Writer's Block" appeared in *College Composition and Communication* in December 1980.

WORKS CITED

Bataille, Robert R. "Hiring Composition Specialists." *WPA: Writing Program Administration*, vol. 4, no. 1, 1980, pp. 17–21.

Blank, Susan, and Beth Greenberg. "Living at the Bottom." *The Radical Teacher*, vol. 5, 1977, pp. 14–16. Reprinted in *WPA: Writing Program Administration*, vol. 5, no.1, 1981, pp. 9–12.

Bonner, Thomas, Jr. "Six Steps Toward Departmental Engagement in Composition." *WPA: Writing Program Administration*, vol. 4, no. 2, 1980, p. 20.

Booth, Wayne C. "A Cheap, Efficient, Challenging, Sure-Fire and Obvious Device for Combatting the Major Scandal in Higher Education Today." *WPA: Writing Program Administration*, vol. 5, no. 1, 1981, pp. 35–40.

Brereton, John. "The Doctorate in Composition at Wayne State University." *Journal of Basic Writing*, vol. 3, no. 2, 1981, pp. 14–22.

Brothers, Barbara. "Three Kinds of Writing Workshops for English Teachers." *WPA: Writing Program Administration*, vol. 4, no. 2, 1980, pp. 21–22.

Comprone, Joseph. "Graduate Programs for Teachers of Basic Writing: The University of Louisville's Ph.D. in Rhetoric and Composition." *Journal of Basic Writing*, vol. 3, no. 2, 1981, pp. 23–45.

Connors, Robert J. *Composition-Rhetoric: Backgrounds, Theory, and Pedagogy*. U of Pittsburgh P, 1997.

Flower, Linda. "Writer-Based Prose: A Cognitive Basis for Problems in Writing." *College English*, vol. 41, no. 1, 1979, pp. 19–37.

Flower, Linda, and John R. Hayes. "The Cognition of Discovery: Defining a Rhetorical Problem." *College Composition and Communication*, vol. 31, no. 1, 1980, pp. 21–32.

Gebhardt, Richard C. "Training Basic Writing Teachers at a Liberal Arts College." *Journal of Basic Writing*, vol. 3, no. 2, 1981, pp. 46–63.

Graves, Richard L., and Harry M. Solomon. "New Graduate Courses in Rhetoric and Composition: A National Survey." *Freshman English News*, vol. 9, no. 1, 1980, p. 1+.

Hairston, Maxine. "What Freshman Directors Need to Know About Evaluating Writing Programs." *WPA: Writing Program Administration*, vol. 3, no. 1, 1979, pp. 11–16.

Larkin, Greg. "The Essential Unity of Language Arts Programs: Its Pedagogical Implications." *WPA: Writing Program Administration*, vol. 3, no. 1, 1979, pp. 25–28.

Lindemann, Erika. "Evaluating Writing Programs: What an Outside Evaluator Looks For." *WPA: Writing Program Administration*, vol. 3, no. 1, 1979, pp. 17–24.

—. Email interview by Lori Ostergaard. 30 Jan. 2018.

Lunsford, Andrea A. "Cognitive Development and the Basic Writer." *College English*, vol. 41, no. 1, 1979, pp. 38–46.

Lyons, Robert. "Faculty Development Through Professional Collaboration." *WPA: Writing Program Administration*, vol. 4, no. 2, 1980, pp. 12–18.

Marius, Richard. "Faculty Indifference to Writing: A Pessimistic View." *WPA: Writing Program Administration*, vol. 4, no. 2, 1980, pp. 7–12.

McClelland, Ben W. "Part-time Faculty in English Composition: A WPA Survey." *WPA: Writing Program Administration*, vol. 5, no. 1, 1981, pp. 13–20.

McQuade, Donald A. "The Case of the Migrant Workers." *WPA: Writing Program Administration*, vol. 5, no. 1, 1981, pp. 29–34.

Moran, Charles. "A Model for Teacher Training Programs in the Field of Writing." *Journal of Basic Writing*, vol. 3, no. 2, 1981, pp. 64–78.

Nold, Ellen. "Helping Faculty Make Rewarding Assignments." *WPA: Writing Program Administration*, vol. 4, no. 2, 1980, p. 19.

Rose, Mike. "Rigid Rules, Inflexible Plans, and the Stifling of Language: A Cognitivist Analysis of Writer's Block." *College Composition and Communication*, vol. 31, no. 4, 1980, pp. 389–401.

Taylor, Karl K. "*Doors* English: The Cognitive Basis of Rhetorical Models." *The Journal of Basic Writing*, vol. 2, no. 2, 1979, pp. 52–66.

Weinman, Geoffrey S. "A Part-Time Freshman Writing Staff: Problems and Solutions." *WPA: Writing Program Administration*, vol. 5, no. 1, 1981, pp. 21–28.

Wiener, Harvey S. "WPA President's Message," *WPA Newsletter*, vol. 1, no. 3, 1978, p. 4.

WPA Board of Consultant Evaluators. "Writing Program Evaluation: An Outline for Self-Study," *WPA: Writing Program Administration*, vol. 4, no. 2, 1980, pp. 23–28.

"WPA Consultation Service." *WPA: Writing Program Administration*, vol. 3, no. 2, 1979, p. 6.

Inez in Transition: Using Case Study to Explore the Experiences of Underrepresented Students in First-Year Composition

Christina Saidy

Abstract

This case study reports on the transition from high school to college writing undertaken by Inez, a first-generation Chicana undergraduate student. Through use of interviews, student writing samples, and research memos, the author illustrates how a seemingly smooth transition to college writing is actually complex and raises questions for WPAs about the ways students—especially underrepresented students—experience the transition to college writing. The author suggests that case studies, like this one, may benefit writing programs, via programmatic assessment and pedagogical modeling.

> *I feel like I'm doing good. I've done so much better. I am happy . . . Because you know at first I felt really, really bad about school in general. It was just like, "No, I don't belong here." But not until the semester has finished I feel so confident about it. I can take on more.*
>
> —"Inez"

Above are the words of Inez,[1] a first-generation Chicana[2] undergraduate student I interviewed for a case study of students in the transition between high school and college writing. Inez made this statement in December of her first semester of college. She had finished her first semester, completed her final exams, and was preparing to head home to spend the winter break with her family. Inez ended the semester on this positive note, confident in her academic performance from the first semester. Inez felt like she'd made it as a writer and as a student. She had learned to negotiate the institution and its expectations. She started to feel like she belonged.

In this article, I share the case study of Inez's transition from high school to college writer. This study examines Inez's perceptions and descriptions of her high school writing experiences, shares how she navigated and transitioned to college writing expectations, and describes her experiences in a first-semester composition course. On the surface, Inez's transition appeared smooth with few hiccups along the way. However, as this case study reveals, writing transitions, especially for students from underrepresented groups, are often complex and political events requiring the writer to successfully navigate institutional policies and barriers, sometimes with support and other times without. For writing program administrators, the close examination of one student's writing transition opens opportunities to consider the role of writing programs and first-year composition (FYC) classes in supporting students, especially first-generation and underrepresented students, in their transitions to college writing.

(Writing) Transitions—Institutional and Programmatic

Broadly, much research has examined the transition to college for Latinx students in the United States. This work has found that Latinx students' success in the transition to college is aided by parental support; personal drive and desire to overcome poverty; college preparatory class work despite initial placement in basic or vocational tracks; and specially designed minority retention and recruitment programs (Falbo, Contreras, and Avalos; Gándara, *Over*). While studies have shown that Latinas, as opposed to their Latino counterparts, are more academically successful in high school and college and graduate at higher rates, gender roles and expectations have the potential to significantly impact these success rates (Gándara, *Making*). Furthermore, students from low socioeconomic or ethnically underrepresented groups who do enroll in college are often less likely to have had access to a college-focused high school curriculum and are often placed in remedial college classes. These factors often lead to less confidence in students' beliefs about their abilities to succeed in college-level work and a feeling that they do not fit, which thus contributes to lower retention rates for Latinx students (Engle and Tinto). In writing programs, the first interaction with students often happens at the moment of placement, long before an incoming student steps on campus. Yet, for students like Inez, this moment can be critical to developing a sense of belonging in both college and the writing class.

Placement is the first interaction between the student and the writing program. Holly Hassel and Joanne Baird Giordano note that placement "is a critical moment of contact—when students are being evaluated for the match between their prior educational experiences and their learning needs as first-semester students" ("Blurry Borders," 60). Furthermore, in writing programs, placement is often shaped by institutional and financial constraints. Hassel and Giordano go on to point out "At many campuses, students are placed into first-year writing courses by standardized placement tests (for example, ACT, SAT, Compass, and Accuplacer) that assess students in limited areas such as usage, grammar, and reading comprehension" (60). In addition to the limited scope of measured skills and abilities for placement in FYC, most standardized tests, such as the SAT and ACT, which was used for Inez's placement, tend to privilege white students from middle and upper-middle-class backgrounds. New research on the SAT in the University of California system found that in a 17-year timespan, race and ethnicity were the largest predictors of standardized test scores with white students scoring significantly higher than black and Latinx students on the SAT (Geiser). This research confirms what composition scholars working in developmental writing and academic retention programs have known for years—standardized tests for placement in writing classes lead to less diverse and often segregated classes. In his *Antiracist Writing Assessment Ecologies*, Asao B. Inoue discusses the remedial early start or bridge courses for students with low scores on California State University's English Placement Test (EPT). Inoue states, "Even a casual look into the classrooms and over the roster of all students in these programs shows a stunning racial picture ... The classes are filled with almost exclusively students of color" (34–35).

WPAs have long understood the impreciseness of standardized tests as placement mechanisms. In their "Toward Writing as Social Justice," Mya Poe and Asao B. Inoue note, "So much of the writing assessment work we do seems complicit in sustaining inequality. No wonder we are drawn to seemingly more democratic assessment methods" (119–20). Among these seemingly more democratic methods, WPAs report exploring placement test replacements such as directed self placement (Royer and Gilles, "Attitude"; Royer and Gilles, *Principles*; Blakesley, Harvey, and Reynolds) and modifications to testing placement (Isaacs and Keohane; Peckham). While these alternate placement methods are often considered more predictive, useful, and just, Hassel and Giordano, citing a report by Fain, note that standardized tests are solely used for placement in 80% of cases ("Blurry Borders," 60). Standardized tests are employed primarily because of budgetary and personnel constraints. However, it is widely accepted that when these tests are used for placement they cannot, or do not, provide the necessary level of sensitivity, especially for students whom standardized testing is known to exclude.

The moment of placement is often a critically important one from a programmatic perspective, since it dictates course numbers, instructional needs, etc. However, this moment is also critically important for students transitioning from high school to college writing because it is the moment in which they are institutionally labeled as prepared or underprepared. A student's writing placement can impact the way the student perceives their abilities, fit in college, and even self-worth. Moreover, Siskanna Naynaha also notes that for traditionally underrepresented students, especially multilingual students, placement or competency exams may "mean they are consigned to a kind of institutional purgatory. They are neither in nor out; they gain access to college but remain blocked from advancement by required courses or chosen programs of study" (197). For students from traditionally underrepresented backgrounds, the moment of placement is often the first time, but certainly not the last time, they experience the gatekeeping aspect of college writing. In her 2004 keynote, "Made Not Only in Words: Composition in a New Key," Kathleen Blake Yancey urged, "Suppose that if instead of focusing on the gatekeeping year, we saw composition education as a *gateway*? Suppose that we enlarged our focus to include *both* moments, gatekeeping and gateway" (306). If we are to heed Yancey's call, to make the first year more than a gatekeeping year, Naynaha argues "unjust placement and curricular models must become the focus of critical inquiry into our institutional practices and especially the ways those practices impact particular student populations" (200). One starting point for this critical inquiry is investigating students' experiences of transition, which includes students' writing backgrounds and experiences and their experiences in our programs. This is information that traditional data sources—test scores, grades, demographic information, and even portfolios of student work—do not provide.

Case Study and the Transitioning Writer

Using case studies for critical inquiry and programmatic fact-finding, research, and assessment offers the opportunity to understand writing transitions, especially for students who are typically underrepresented in our institutions. Case studies are in-depth studies of individual representatives of a group, organizations, or phenomena in the natural context (Hancock and Algozzine). Case studies do not typically provide generalizable findings. Rather, they provide stories and real examples that raise additional questions about decision-making and practice (Dyson and Genishi; Yin). For WPAs, case studies offer an additional layer of information to consider in institutional and programmatic assessment. Although case studies may only reflect the experiences of one person at a time, they offer us glimpses into the student's experience of our programs that we typically cannot obtain from other types of data available to us such as grades, retention rates, student academic indicators, course evaluations, or even student portfolios.

Case studies ranging from anecdotal stories to more formal uses of the methodology have a history in FYC for offering a picture of what writing classrooms look like. For example, in his 1989 book *Lives on the Boundary*, Mike Rose uses anecdotes to represent students who, "By the various criteria the institutions use . . . deserve admission—but they are considered marginal, 'high risk' or 'at risk' in current administrative parlance. 'The truly illiterate among us,' was how one dean described them" (2). Rose goes on to show that the specific students he describes, those placed into the university's lowest level writing course, are as one might assume of students accepted into a competitive university, highly intellectual and critical thinkers who are both aware of their placement and struggle with feelings of inadequacy because of it.

In recent years, these anecdotal accounts have been enhanced by research that focuses on using case study methodologies to further provide insight into the academic and cultural experiences of students in writing transitions. For example, in his book *Transiciones*, Todd Ruecker follows language minority students from high school into college and offers suggestions for ways that writing programs and institutions can better serve underrepresented and language minority students. In his article "From Journals to Journalism," Kevin Roozen tracked a writer from a college bridge program, through college writing and college, and into a career in journalism. Roozen explored ways that the student's personal journals were significant in her writing transitions. The work of Ruecker and Roozen have begun to illustrate the role of case study in exploring writing transitions, especially for students who are traditionally considered underrepresented in university settings. My case study of Inez adds further complexity to discussions of writing transitions, writing placement, and the institutional and political considerations WPAs face as they address these transitions.

As a case study researcher, it is important to disclose my own subjectivity. My interest in Inez and in her transformation as a writer is rooted in my experience as a former secondary English language arts teacher and FYC instructor, and now as an assistant professor of English teaching writing methods courses for secondary teachers and as a writing researcher examining writing transitions from secondary school to college. My research focuses on complex stories of writing transitions as a way to influence the field's thinking about institutional policies and practice. However, this interest is also informed by my personal transition into college and college writing. Like Inez, I was a first-generation college student. My father, an immigrant from Brazil, had a high school education, and my mother, a white woman born and raised in the United States, graduated high school and then attended technical school when I was a child. After technical school, she had a successful career in healthcare, but she had no formal college education. My parents very much wanted me to attend college, and I did. Like Inez, I remember throughout college feeling on and off like I did not belong. Fortunately, I participated in a college bridge and retention program for students like me at UCLA: first-generation college students, underrepresented students, and students from low-income families. I often credit that program and its academic and community support system for keeping me in college.

As a researcher, I am aware that stories like mine and Inez's are often told in aggregate form. Our experiences of education are typically reduced to statistics about postsecondary success and retention or, on the flip side, postsecondary attrition and dropout rates. Therefore, as a university researcher and teacher committed to understanding writing transitions, I believe it is important to contribute work that is reflective of the nuance, complexity, and detail of writers' experiences as they transition from high school to college and that accurately reflect people, experiences, and institutional policies/practices that help or hinder students. In addition to understanding the statistical norms and outliers that constitute data about writing programs, it is important to continue adding real examples and stories that impact programmatic and institutional decision-making and change.

In the following pages, I will share Inez's story. At the most basic level, her story represents the experience of one Chicana student and her writing transition as she enters a large public university. I will use Inez's story to raise questions and make observations about her experience. Furthermore, I will argue that Inez's case, while only one student's experience, invites us to consider case studies as a form of programmatic fact-finding and assessment. This form of assessment encourages us to engage in critical inquiry that serves students, strengthens teaching, and provides information about who and how programs serve or fail to serve their students, especially traditionally underrepresented students.

Learning about Inez

To learn about Inez's transition to college writing, I met with her monthly from August to December of her first year of college. I collected a pre-survey in August and post-survey in December. At each monthly meeting, I interviewed Inez. These interviews were voice recorded. They lasted anywhere from 20–45 minutes. Inez was an engaging interviewee, and she shared very openly with me. She told me on more than one occasion that she liked being involved in "the research" and asked questions about my research methods, practices, and areas. I collected copies of all Inez's writing assignments from her first semester writing course. I invited Inez to bring her writing from her composition class to our interviews and each time she would read a passage to me. This would give us the opportunity to talk about her writing choices and progress, and it would help me to understand the elements of her writing that were most important or interesting to her. Finally, at the end of each interview session, I wrote research memos. The purpose of the research memos was twofold: (1) they were a reflective practice for me, and (2) Inez would often continue talking as we walked to the copy machine to copy her assignments or prior to leaving my office. Often, I learned much about Inez, her family, and her experiences from these side conversations that were not voice recorded, and I used my memos to keep track of these added details. At the end of our meetings, I kept in touch with Inez via email.

I recruited Inez for participation in my study from her high school. Inez attended an urban high school in the Southwest that I call Community High School. Prior to meeting Inez, I had conducted research and provided professional development to teachers at Community High School. The school currently enrolls 1,800–2,000 students yearly. The school population is comprised of 94% Latinx/Chicanx students, 2% Anglo, 2.5% African American, and 0.8% Native American students. Some 89% to 94% of students receive free and reduced lunch. The school reports a four-year graduation rate of 66.2% percent. Out of Community High's graduating class, 11% plan to obtain a postsecondary education. The majority of these students attend local community colleges. In the year I recruited Inez into the study, approximately 15 students planned to attend the nearest state university. Through my work at Community High School, it became evident that even the school's highest achievers were often labeled at-risk or underprepared when they entered college, and I wanted to understand why.

Inez is a first-generation college student, but not the first in her family to enroll in postsecondary education. Inez's older sister attended a local community college until she became pregnant and needed to work longer hours to support her son. Inez's parents are both immigrants from Mexico. Her father immigrated to California as a teenager and attended high school in California for a short time where he learned English. Inez's mother graduated from high school in Mexico before immigrating to Arizona. Inez's parents met and married in the United States and Inez, her older sister, and her younger brother were all born in Arizona. The family primarily speaks Spanish at home. However, all Inez's education has been in English. She was never classified as an English-language learner in school and all schooled reading and writing has been in English since kindergarten. Inez's father works as custodial staff at a local college, and her mother works as housekeeping staff at a large hotel. Inez's mother is a union activist, and her sister has become an activist as well. Inez told me a number of stories of working on activist campaigns alongside her mother and sister. Her mother, who is not a citizen, is very active in registering community members to vote.

Inez chose to attend the in-state, local university, Southwest State University, primarily for financial reasons. She qualified for financial aid, and her parents were able to help her pay for the costs of schooling and housing not covered in her aid package. Southwest State is the state's largest public university. As part of its mission, Southwest State seeks to increase access to postsecondary education for traditionally underrepresented students, including Latinx students. In the semester Inez entered Southwest State, approximately 18.5% of the student population identified at Chicanx/Latinx, while the state Chicanx/Latinx population in the same year was 31% (*Demographic*).

Upon admission to Southwest State, Inez declared a criminal justice major since she planned to go to law school. Her parents were excited that Inez wanted to be a lawyer. However, before even beginning her freshman year of college, Inez changed her major to psychology when realized she did not want to be a lawyer. At the midpoint of the first semester, Inez once again changed her major, this time to elementary education. On her "About Me" page of her online writing portfolio, Inez states: "My passion is children. I want to pursue a career as a teacher. I want to teach 3rd graders. After I have had the experience, I eventually want to work my way up into becoming a principal." Inez told me that another motivating factor for becoming a teacher is that her younger brother, who is in elementary school, has had trouble in school and she is interested in helping students in the way she wants her brother to be helped.

Writing in High School—Success and Support

Inez started her high school career in what she called "normal" English. At Inez's school, normal or regular English was the class for students who were not tracked into honors. However, early on, Inez was moved to the honors class. She said, "I started in normal English, but then the teacher thought that I would be good in honors." Although Inez's teacher perceived her writing and reading abilities to be above average performance, Inez was at first insecure in the honors track. She told me, "When I took that leap into honors I felt really discouraged by everybody just because they wrote wonderful papers. I really had something simple. That was the awkwardness about being in honors. Either you were too smart to be normal, or I felt too dumb to be in honors." Despite Inez's insecurities about her writing and fit in the honors track, she reports excelling in her high school classes, especially English language arts. On more than one occasion Inez said that high school was easy or that she didn't have to work very hard. Inez's hard work on writing in school was rewarded with good grades. She received A's in language arts every semester. Inez's early experience as a writer in high school was shaped by her teacher's perception of her writing as honors-level material. This teacher's act of moving Inez to honors greatly shaped her experience of learning to write in high school because she remained tracked in more challenging writing courses throughout her high school experience.

To be successful in high school, Inez regularly completed "A lot of independent writing where it was just like, write about this and that. We had to write five pages every time." She noted that most of the writing topics were things she did not care about, or topics she did not choose, and that often papers would be returned with just a grade and no comments. Inez told me that she completed the five-page writing assignments easily and regularly. Although Inez wrote regularly and at length in her English language arts honors classes, writing was minimal in classes outside of English. Inez reports doing PowerPoints in biology but no sustained writing in classes other than English. This supports Applebee and Langer's findings that writing in high school classes is minimal and that, on average, students write 2.1 pages per week of writing combined in social studies, math, and science. The majority of this writing is fill-in-the-blanks (15).

When asked what mattered most in her high school writing, Inez noted, "That we didn't plagiarize . . . Just that it [the writing] was ours. That it was our opinion. That's what was valued the most." Inez told me that writing original work in high school was easy, which is part of the overall picture of her high school writing experience. In high school, Inez wrote regularly, by senior year five pages at a time, and was rewarded with high marks on her assignments. Although she did not necessarily receive detailed feedback on her writing, she met the ethical expectations for writing in high school and grew beyond her ninth-grade lack of confidence to feel like a fairly successful writer.

During her high school years, Inez also developed into a successful writer outside of school. She told the story:

> There was this one time in my junior year. I volunteered for political campaigning. I wrote an essay just on what I thought about it. The person that I worked for in the campaign, she loved it so much that she cancelled somebody else's speech and she put me in there.

Writing in this particular context brought together the family commitment to politics and campaigning and Inez's schooled strengths. Furthermore, this experience of being publically selected to share writing solidified Inez's confidence in her writing abilities. Although Inez started high school feeling apprehensive about being on the honors track, she developed into a successful and confident writer both inside and outside of school.

Placement and the Institution

When Inez entered college, her confidence in her writing quickly faded. Because of her ACT score, Inez was placed into Stretch writing, a course that stretches the first composition course (English 101) over two semesters. The first-semester course is counted as an elective course and students take English 101 in the spring semester of their first year and English 102 in the fall of their second year. The Stretch course is intended to give struggling writers more writing practice and to increase retention rates.

Inez saw her placement in Stretch as a misunderstanding of institutional structures. For example, she told me, "My ACT score was 17. I was put in [Stretch English]." When she talked about the ACT, she said, "We thought it was a required test. We didn't know it would affect us in college, so we didn't really try, or I didn't. If I could go back I'd probably try." Inez's comments point out some of the challenges of using standardized tests for placement. In our standardized testing culture, students learn not to take tests all that seriously since they are regularly evaluated formally. Furthermore, as Hassel and Giordano point out, using standardized tests for placement often leads to incorrect placement of students who do not test well ("Blurry Borders"; "Transfer Institutions"). Research shows that SAT and ACT tests privileges white, affluent males and that women, black and Latinx students, and students from lower socioeconomic backgrounds regularly test lower (Geiser and Studley). There is no way to know whether Inez could have tried harder and done better, but this particular placement mechanism made her feel, in her words "lower about my writing." She goes on to say, "I think the idea of being in that class discouraged all of us because we felt like, I guess dumb in a way." While the Stretch course was designed to increase retention and give Inez extra practice, she saw it as remedial and an indicator that she was not good enough for the institution.

Although Inez saw her placement as a mark of her deficits as a test taker and writer, she was also aware of the political implications of placement. In talking about her Stretch course she told me, "When I go in there, basically all you see is nothing but minorities. We're all either Hispanic and one African American girl. It makes me feel like we're all . . . Here's all the Hispanic people for [State University]." I was not able to confirm the ethnic makeup of Inez's class, but I was impacted by Inez's perception of her experience and clear articulation of the students who made up her class.

Becoming a College Writer

As a writer, Inez excelled in her Stretch writing class. She maintained an A grade the entire semester, and her final grade in the course was a 96%. Inez's writing was well received by the instructor and by fellow students in her writing class. In a sense, the Stretch class was the first time that Inez's schooled writing became public in a number of ways. Inez told me that in high school she never received feedback on her writing. She suspected her writing teachers did not really read her writing, and she never read other students writing via peer review. This contrasted dramatically with Inez's experience in college in which it was clear that her teacher read her writing and she often shared writing with her classmates as part of the composition process. What impacted Inez most was her teacher often asking if she could share aloud Inez's writing with the rest of the class. In this writing, Inez was invited to write about her experiences and things she cared about deeply. In one of these examples, Inez wrote:

> I grew up in the Hispanic community. I only spoke English in class. I used to get grounded for speaking English at home. Going to Mexico is really funny because here I am such a Mexican. I eat Mexican food, I have dark skin, my height is 4'11", and I have trouble pronouncing certain words. I've been yelled at to get out of this country. How can I leave my own country? I was born here. Just because Mexican blood runs through my veins, I am not American enough? When I go to Mexico I am considered a Gringa. Why? Because I love country music, I don't really eat real Mexican food, and I'm rich over here. It's really hard finding who you really are in a world where society characterizes you based on appearance."

After the teacher read this aloud, Inez reports a classmate turned to her and said, "Whoa. That was deep. You wrote that?" In the passage, Inez interrogated what it means to belong, which is something she struggled with in her personal life, transition to college writing, and transition to the university more broadly. Furthermore, Inez appreciated the attention that came from being recognized for her writing, and this helped her to see that writing for an audience gave her writing a sense of purpose.

Deficits and Belonging

Throughout the semester, Inez was successful in her writing class, and toward the end of the semester, Inez was able to express a sense of accomplishment and feeling that she had made it by learning how to negotiate her writing transition and, more broadly, her university transition. Furthermore, as the semester progressed, the topic of Inez's placement in Stretch came up, in some way, every time we met. However, the discussion of Inez's placement changed dramatically. Inez's early description of the students in her writing class showed a critical awareness of the racial politics of tracking and sorting and a sense of anger and injustice about institutional policies and practices to which she did not have access. However, beginning in the middle of the semester, her anger was quickly replaced with shrinking confidence in her abilities as a writer. She told me that placement in the Stretch course made her feel "lower about [her] writing" and went on to say, "I think the idea of being in that class discouraged all of us because we felt like, I guess, dumb in a way." Inez left high school a successful writer who regularly wrote on demand up to five pages at a time. Yet, as a result of her placement, a placement she did not completely understand, she began to feel dumb and lower.

As the semester went on, Inez's feelings of inadequacy transformed. She enjoyed her writing class, and she felt successful since she shared her writing with other students via peer review, was invited to write about things that *mattered* to her, and had her writing read aloud to the class by her instructor. However, as Inez's personal feelings about the class became more positive, the way she represented her work became more problematic. Inez began to internalize the deficit that she resisted at her initial placement. For example, in our November interview, Inez justified her placement saying, "They told me I had to take the class for a reason, you know?" Later that day, as we walked to the copy machine, Inez told me that her instructor told the students how important the Stretch class was and that students who took that class often passed English 102 at higher rates than students who did not take the class. Inez had come to trust her instructor and how the instructor valued her writing, so too Inez came to trust the instructor's defense of the course as supportive of Inez's future writing success.

Furthermore, Inez often talked about how students from her community were slower or behind. She told me academic reading and writing takes me longer, I think, because I'm exposed to new vocabulary that I wasn't used to back in my community. It's a lot of new vocabulary that I know I'm expected to know by my age but since I haven't had practice in it, I am a little slower at it. I'm getting there. I'm trying.

Inez focused on a perceived cultural deficit and assumption that she is missing knowledge because of her experience with language and her cultural background. Inez's experience of internalizing her deficits operates separate from her success in her writing class and separate from the fact that introductory college-level reading and writing is challenging for many students. Inez stopped seeing her placement as a function of her missing institutional knowledge and began seeing it as a function of her deficient writing skills and abilities.

Asking Questions, Seeing Gaps

On the surface, Inez made a successful transition to college writing. She came to college as an accomplished and successful high school writer and continued that success in her FYC class by finishing the class with a high grade and feeling accomplished as a writer. If I had only looked at Inez's test scores, demographics, grades, and a portfolio of her work, I would assume that Inez's transition was smooth and uncomplicated. Yet, through my case study, I came to see Inez's story as a more complex and nuanced story about the politics and experiences of placement and the transition to college writing for a student who was traditionally underrepresented at my university. Case studies, such as my study of Inez, offer an additional layer of information about students that complements existing teaching and programmatic assessment materials such as test scores, grades, course evaluations, and student portfolios.

Inez had been tracked and sorted throughout her academic career. In high school, she was tracked into honors based on abilities perceived by her teachers. Inez's comments about honors and normal English language arts show a sophisticated understanding of the ways tracking and sorting work. Furthermore, Inez seemed aware that what constituted honors at her urban high school may have been different than honors in other schools where students had socioeconomic privilege. Inez's experience of tracking and sorting changed dramatically when she was placed, via test scores, into the Stretch course. Inez believed that her placement, which she perceived as a remedial, was the function of missing institutional knowledge and a lack of understanding regarding the role of standardized testing in college placement processes. While Inez did not link this missing institutional knowledge to standardized test biases, she did clearly note that her Stretch course was primarily comprised of students with similar ethnic backgrounds as hers, and she expressed great disappointment that "all of the brown kids" would be in a class she considered remedial.

As in many writing programs, the large program at Southwest State University relies solely on test scores for placement. Funds are not provided for other placement measures, and the writing program's courses are typically filled to capacity at the beginning of the semester, which limits the mobility of students who may have been misplaced. These institutional constraints, paired with the political implication of using standardized testing for placement seem to be the perfect recipe for the type of segregation Inez described.

Case studies have the potential to raise questions and provide rich description to evaluate student experience and learning in situations where institutional constraints impact programmatic practice and decision-making. For example, the early data from the initial implementation of the Stretch program showed that the demographics of the classes matched the university's demographics. However, Inez's comments about all the brown kids in the room counters this early data and suggests that a closer examination of the segregation in these classes may be warranted. A 2008 Pell report by Jennifer Engle and Vincent Tinto finds that first-year college students from underrepresented groups who are placed in remedial classes are more likely to drop out of school because they feel they do not belong. Rather than dropping out, Inez attempted to understand her placement and the necessity of the Stretch course. In doing so, Inez internalized deficits related to writing ability, which she did not actually seem to have. If the Stretch courses are disproportionately comprised of "the brown kids" as Inez perceived, are they actually increasing retention? If so, at what cost? Using case studies for programmatic assessment has the potential to make questions and programmatic concerns visible in ways that retention data, such as grades and percentages, cannot.

Case Study as Instructional Complement

While case studies certainly have the potential to raise programmatic questions, an added benefit of the case study approach was Inez's informal learning about university research, writing, and even publishing. Inez regularly asked me about my research and writing. She wanted to understand how it worked and why it worked that way. She saw connections between the interviews she conducted for the research for her writing class and the case study research I was doing. While I was not Inez's instructor, it was empowering for her to think that her experience could impact the way instructors,

WPAs, and university-level administrators think about a writing program. Through the case study, I came to see that Inez saw me as a form of literacy sponsor (Brandt). Via this case study methodology, Inez, a student who was struggling to navigate the university and its practices, felt integrated into the research that is integral to the way her university works.

In her "Definitive Article on Class Size," Alice Horning notes that the small size of composition courses adds to student engagement and learning, offers space for in-depth writing process activities since teachers have time to respond to many drafts of writing, and contributes to higher retention rates for incoming students. Because of the familiarity between instructors and students in the FYC course, students have the opportunity to see their instructors not only as subject matter experts in composition but also as researchers and learners who are continually developing. Integrating case studies into individual practice is one way for FYC instructors to model research for their developing writers who are also conducting research and to develop a deep understanding of their students in the transition to college writing.

In programs where a large number of graduate teaching assistants take responsibility for teaching FYC courses, a case study model could both benefit the program, the graduate students' research, and the FYC students who are case study subjects. For example, case studies could be assigned in the writing practicum to help developing TAs to learn about their students in order to directly impact curriculum and retention. For programs with graduate-level, WPA-focused seminars, this methodology can be used in a semester-long programmatic assessment. This helps future WPAs learn a specific method for qualitative research while also learning how to regularly conduct in-depth programmatic assessments on a continuing basis. Finally, in programs that use portfolio assessment for direct assessment of student writing, case studies may offer a way to complement, or even replace, student portfolios. For example, throughout the semester, Inez's portfolio showed that she was an accomplished writer. However, the additional information I gathered about her gave context to her placement, class work, and the overall experience of writing in FYC that I could not have gleaned from her work alone.

The integration of case studies into the work of writing program instructors and graduate students also invite instructors to see ways that assessment, as Staci M. Perryman-Clark notes, "creates or denies opportunity structures" (206). At Southwest State, as in many programs across the country, faculty in writing programs are often far less diverse than students taking their classes. Perryman-Clark argues that to support students of color and linguistically diverse students,

> white, monolingual instructors and graduate students are challenged to work differently from the practices to which they have been accustomed, and by working differently, white, monolingual instructors and graduate students often see themselves as unsure of what exactly they should do. (210)

Integrating case studies into the work of writing instructors and graduate students opens up the opportunity to more clearly see and address the institutional and pedagogical elements that deny opportunity structures in order to consider ways to better support traditionally underrepresented students and create opportunity structures.

Conclusion

Case studies open up opportunities to understand the experiences and writing development of students who are often misunderstood by other measures. As Mya Poe and Asao B. Inoue remind us, "So much of the writing assessment work we do seems complicit in sustaining inequality" (119) and Inez's story confirms this. Inez was highly ranked out of high school but, according to her test scores, at risk in FYC. Via this case study, I want to suggest that transitioning writers like Inez have much to teach us about programmatic policies, practices, and assessment in our programs. The integration of case study methodology offers an opportunity for instructors to conduct research alongside their students, get to know these students and their stories of transition more deeply, and alter instruction to meet the needs of transitioning writers. Case studies offer programs a way to develop a deep understanding of their students, especially their traditionally underrepresented students, via data that can be used to complement, or even challenge, traditional and more quantitative data sources that are typically used in writing programs or by upper level university administrators.

Notes

1. The names of all people and institutions appearing in this article are pseudonyms. This research was institutional review board (IRB) approved.

2. I am using the term Chicana specifically to describe Inez's ethnicity and the gender-neutral Chicanx or Latinx in situations where I am speaking generally. At the beginning of the case study, Inez used Chicana, Hispanic, and Mexican interchangeably to describe herself, as evidenced by her writing samples. However, as the semester moved on, and she continued in a Chicanx studies class, Inez began using Chicana when talking about her ethnicity. Therefore, to honor Inez's own choice of language, I use Chicana when I am specifically writing about her.

Works Cited

Applebee, Arthur N., and Judith A. Langer. "A Snapshot of Writing Instruction in Middle Schools and High Schools." *English Journal*, vol. 100, no. 6, 2011, pp. 14–27.

Blakesley, David, Erin J. Harvey, and Erica J. Reynolds. "Southern Illinois University Carbondale as an Institutional Model: The English 100/101 Stretch and Directed Self-placement Program." Royer and Gilles, *Directed*, pp. 207–41.

Brandt, Deborah. "Sponsors of Literacy." *College Composition and Communication*, vol. 49, no. 2, 1998, pp. 165–85.

Demographic and Economic Profiles of Hispanics by State and County, 2014. Pew Research Center, www.pewhispanic.org/states.

Dyson, Anne Haas, and Celia Genishi. *On the Case: Approaches to Language and Literacy Research*. Teachers College P, 2005.

Engle, Jennifer, and Vincent Tinto. "Moving Beyond Access: College Success for Low-Income, First-Generation Students." Pell Institute for the Study of Opportunity in Higher Education, 2008, pellinstitute.org/downloads/publications-Moving_Beyond_Access_2008.pdf.

Falbo, Toni, Helen Contreras, and Maria D. Avalos. "Transition Points from High School to College." *Latinos in Higher Education*, edited by David J. León, Emerald Group Publishing, 2003, pp. 59–72. Diversity in Higher Education 3.

Gándara, Patricia C. *Over the Ivy Walls: The Educational Mobility of Low-Income Chicanos*. State U of New York P, 1995.

—. *Making Education Work for Latinas in the US*. UCLA: The Civil Rights Project / Proyecto Derechos Civiles, 2013, civilrightsproject.ucla.edu/research/college-access/underrepresented-students/making-education-work-for-latinas-in-the-u.s/gandara-longoria-report-2014.pdf.

Geiser, Saul. "The Growing Correlation Between Race and SAT Scores: New Findings from California." *Center for Studies in Higher Education Research and Occasional Paper Series*, vol. 10, no.15, 2015, pp. 1–43.

Geiser, Saul, and Roger Studley. "UC and the SAT: Predictive Validity and Differential Impact of the SAT I and SAT II at the University of California." *Educational Assessment*, vol. 8, no. 1, 2002, pp. 1–26.

Hancock, Dawson R., and Bob Algozzine. *Doing Case Study Research: A Practical Guide for Beginning Researchers*. Teachers College P, 2011.

Hassel, Holly, and Joanne Baird Giordano. "The Blurry Borders of College Writing: Remediation and the Assessment of Student Readiness." *College English*, vol. 78 no. 1, 2015, pp. 56–80.

—. "Transfer Institutions, Transfer of Knowledge: The Development of Rhetorical Adaptability and Underprepared Writers." *Teaching English in the Two-Year College*, vol. 37, no. 1, 2009, pp. 24–40.

Horning, Alice. "The Definitive Article on Class Size." *WPA: Writing Program Administration*, vol. 31, nos. 1–2, 2007, pp. 11–34.

Inoue, Asao B. *Antiracist Writing Assessment Ecologies: Teaching and Assessing Writing for a Socially Just Future.* WAC Clearinghouse / Parlor P, 2015, wac.colostate.edu/books/inoue/ecologies.pdf

Isaacs, Emily, and Catherine Keohane. "Writing Placement That Supports Teaching and Learning." *WPA: Writing Program Administration*, vol. 35, no. 2, 2012, pp. 55–84.

Naynaha, Siskanna. "Assessment, Social Justice, and Latinxs in the US Community College." *College English*, vol. 79, no. 2, 2016, pp. 196–201.

Peckham, Irvin. "Online Placement in First-Year Writing." *College Composition and Communication*, vol. 60, no. 3, 2009, pp. 517–40.

Perryman-Clark, Staci M. "Who We Are(n't) Assessing: Racializing Language and Writing Assessment in Writing Program Administration." *College English*, vol. 79, no. 2, 2016, pp. 206–11.

Poe, Mya, and Asao B. Inoue. "Toward Writing as Social Justice: An Idea Whose Time Has Come." *College English*, vol. 79, no. 2, 2016, pp. 119–26.

Rose, Mike. *Lives on the Boundary: The Struggles and Achievements of America's Underprepared*, The Free P, 1989.

Roozen, Kevin. "From Journals to Journalism: Tracing Trajectories of Literate Development." *College Composition and Communication*, vol. 60, no. 3, 2009, pp. 541–72.

Royer, Daniel J., and Roger Gilles. "Directed Self-Placement: An Attitude of Orientation." *College Composition and Communication*, vol. 50, no. 1, 1998, pp. 54–70.

—. *Directed Self-Placement: Principles and Practices.* Hampton P, 2003.

Ruecker, Todd. "Transiciones: Pathways of Latinas and Latinos Writing in High School and College." Utah State UP, 2015.

Yancey, Kathleen Blake. "Made Not Only in Words: Composition in a New Key." *College Composition and Communication*, no. 56, vol. 2, 2004, pp. 297–328.

Yin, Robert K. *Case Study Research: Design And Methods.* Sage Publications, 2013.

Christina Saidy is assistant professor of English at Arizona State University. Her research focuses on writing and writing transitions with secondary students, teachers in professional development groups, and students entering college.

Making (Collective) Memory Public: WPA Histories in Dialogue

Kelly Ritter

ABSTRACT

This article calls for WPAs to undertake a dialogic archiving of their various individual and program histories. While periodic aggregated information about WPA local practices has been included in our field scholarship—from Warner Taylor's 1929 survey to the 2015 National Census of Writing—where writing program work has been recorded and subsequently analyzed as a data set, there has yet to be a deeper engagement with the sometimes opposing concepts of memory and history. Examining the implications of distinguishing between those two concepts as has been articulated in recent rhetorical theory, I make the case for a renewed attention to capturing and embracing collective memory in our ongoing archives of practice in writing program administration.

> While we sit solemnly in smoke-filled hotel rooms in St. Louis and quibble about the relative merits of composition and communication programs or the latest developments in the upper stratosphere of linguistics research, many of our students are waging a desperate fight against early academic death . . . Most of us, I am sure, come to these meetings to find out how we can best help these students. These meetings are really worthwhile only insofar as they enable us to return to our desks and face that pile of themes with greater equanimity and confidence that we handle them properly. All else is sound and fury signifying nothing.
>
> —Charles Roberts,
> "A Course for Training Rhetoric Teachers at the University of Illinois"(193)

Thanks to twenty-first century technologies, writing program administrators now have the means to dialogue in venues that transcend the conditions of the 1954 CCCC meeting described above. WPAs are furthermore acutely aware of the importance of understanding and mirroring practices and policies on a cross-institutional basis, so as to effectively respond to—or combat—national educational initiatives that threaten local expertise in the teaching of writing, and to share best practices that will advance the livelihoods of writing faculty and students. Yet, our ability to locate these many conversations, remembrances, and cross-articulations of theory into practice in a singular, dynamic place that is not dependent upon our ongoing presence, or an incomplete archive, remains unrealized, despite significant attempts to make the work of WPAs visible to both internal and external publics.

Historically, the "conversations" had by WPAs have been conducted with best intentions, but often lacking the context and conditions allowing us to react to and act upon them. Budgets permitting, we meet at conferences for a few precious days per year. Many of us participate in open electronic conversations such as the WPA listserv, others in more selective chats on social media or in regional groups or affiliated networks. But in many of these conversations—particularly those happening online—we are still talking past and through each other, with an unreliable or unevenly archived record of what was said, let alone a record of how utterances altered or incited responsive practices. In contrast, we robustly *individually* articulate, and sometimes also archive, our practices in micro, local contexts: in department meetings, staff training, campus-wide presentations, and program policy statements, and even in our field publications, on a wider scale. Yet these articulations are rarely put into real-time conversation with other happenings on other campuses; they are ultimately siloed archives that neither intersect nor interact. When we record our remembrances and conversations in scholarship—in annals of disciplinary history—it is too often fragmented across both venue and time, especially given digital aggregators and search engines that allow articles to stand apart from their original context of publication and the orbiting conversations represented therein.

In order to fully articulate the personal and professional decisions which have affected a WPA's own local writing program as well as to archive the institutional *responses* to those decisions and the larger conversation(s) that informed them, WPAs need to build and robustly contribute to a site for cross-institutional dialogues of theory and practice, one including remembrances that showcase our professional ethics as well as our personal biases. We as a WPA community need to engage in *collective memory*, in the rhetorical sense, in conceptualizing such a project, so as to effectively integrate our grand narratives, local histories, and individual portraits. In doing so, we can draw upon theories of memory that both illuminate how we might approach memorializing our conversations and how basic historical recovery does not itself constitute a collective remembrance. We must aggregate our histories both for the posterity of that aggregation, and for the opportunity to see them together, and grow them dynamically over time. We must not be satisfied with just occasions for lament and complaint that immediately erase themselves, such as those at the 1954 convention; we instead must be willing to challenge and add to one another's local practices as memorialized and historicized in a more public, global sense.

I thus argue here for a reconceptualization of the recording, remembering, and re-animating of our WPA practices, histories, and stories. First, I discuss relevant theories of memory—including distinctions between individual and collective—that come from rhetorical theory and that inform a more holistic aggregation of and dialogue about WPA practices. I then briefly discuss three notable instantiations of WPA practice as aggregated and disseminated to the field, appearing across the last eighty years, as examples of archiving that approaches but falls short (to varying degrees) of a fully dialogic experience about the history and practice of WPA work. Finally, I offer suggestions for how a more robust, dialogic presence of WPA programmatic interactions might be enacted as a large-scale project, and why that enactment is both difficult under present conceptions of what constitutes scholarship for those evaluating the work of WPAs, and yet critical to WPAs' ongoing professional work.

Rhetorical Memory: Affordances for WPA Histories of Practice

There are many ways to theoretically ground an argument such as the one I am making. Wrapped in it are issues of how and what we remember as WPAs; how we record, track, and learn from those memories; and how, as a field, we value the practice of remembering and historicizing our practices in order to allow the local archive to enter a national conversation. While I recognize that one of the acute obstacles to a mass kind of practice-centered remembrance for WPAs is the labor and motivations that are sometimes absent—issues I return to in my conclusion—I believe that the strongest theoretical basis for understanding and subsequently moving forward with a site for WPA collective memory is found in theories of individual versus collective remembering, which come in their most germane form from scholars in rhetorical theory.

To first ground the problem in what we *have* done as a field toward remembering our histories, I would point to many archival studies of individual WPAs and programs, of which readers are likely aware. These have been growing in number over the last twenty-five years, starting arguably with Brereton's *The Origins of Composition* and moving more recently toward collections such as L'Eplattenier and Mastrangelo's *Historical Studies of Writing Program Administration,* Ramsey et. al's *Working in the Archives,* Gold and Hobbs' *Educating the New Southern Woman,* and Ostergaard and Wood's *In the Archives of Composition* (which highlights an archive even less fully recovered, that of normal schools). There is no question that WPA histories are ripe for historicizing, nor that WPAs of earlier generations deserve to have their voices recovered. In response to this, alongside compendiums of WPA histories, we have also seen monographs focusing more narrowly on a particular WPA or program (see for example Henze, Selzer, and Sharer; Gold, *Rhetoric at the Margins*; Lamos; Ritter, *Before Shaughnessy* and *To Know Her Own History*; Skinnell; and Soliday). In this research, keen attention has been paid to the recovery of local practices as they inform our present activities, on a scale, and our conceptions of how writing, as a subject, has been drawn and delivered in US colleges and universities. And for this attention, we have been rewarded: archival studies of writing programs have in recent years dominated the CCCC best book award, and have also been well represented in conferences and settings outside the CCCC and the annual CWPA conference.

Yet, despite our significant interest in local recovery projects, we have been unable to gather these histories of practice in any kind of comprehensive or dialogic way. Indeed, one of the first pieces of scholarship that lays claim to being *a* "history" of writing program administration—Edward P.J. Corbett's 1993 collection honoring Winifred Bryan Horner—is not really a history at all in the comprehensive sense of practice. Corbett—who of course famously asserted that there was no such thing as a WPA prior to around World War II—postulates that the "closest thing we have" to a WPA history is Susan Miller's 1991 *Textual Carnivals*—a book that, arguably, neither deeply archives WPA work nor engages in primarily historiographic methods to make its arguments (61). Corbett offers a professional-personal history of writing program administration that is actually a wide (if not sweeping) history of *writing* as taught and received at US colleges and universities from the late nineteenth century onward, including a brief discussion of the CCCC and a naming of twenty to thirty big players in this history. But this in no way could be construed as a true history of writing program *administration,* even as we, as scholars, often blur the subject and the supervision versus structure of its curricular delivery. There are no wide-scale, *intersecting* stories of WPAs, no discussion of how or why programs have come to be designed, no interrogation of the political position(s) of WPAs among faculty. And importantly, there is no attention paid to *how* or *why* we remember and archive our practices; that is neither his goal nor his project.

Certainly, Corbett's history is indicative of how, in the early 1990s, we longed for histories of this kind, even on this scale, to be made public as an interpretation of grand narratives—as evidence proving our field *was* a field. The desire for rhetoric and composition to exist as a legitimate discipline is strongly tied to how that presence will be sustained, and later retold. But Corbett's narrative is also indicative of the struggle to gather our individual histories into a meaningful dialogue that does not rely on the valorization or emphasis of particular actors, or the in-depth study of particular programs. We contextualize our histories, but we do not allow them to talk with (or even about) one another. We *record* our practices through various instruments of large-scale aggregation—as I will discuss later—but we do not personalize or annotate those for future readers, or for the WPAs who will inherit our programs, through considerations of practices of memorialization or the effect memory has on what we aim to build or dismantle in our programmatic work. We have memories, but they are not collective ones. We are public, but we are not *a* public.

Our lacking collective memory can be partly blamed on the fact that many WPAs today work in relative isolation within their institutions, unable to discuss their practices and compare their memories (and recover what they have forgotten) with colleagues, let alone theorize how these practices might be archived in a larger context for a variety of field uses. We WPAs have varied resources at our disposal, and as such, have differing stakes and roles in the national "conversation" governing and guiding administrative work in writing programs. Yet thinking about a theoretical foundation for how such archiving might be approached is necessary in considering such an archive at all. For this purpose, I turn to rhetorical studies, specifically scholarship focusing on memory and publics, to illustrate how both the ongoing work of WPAs and the methods by which that work might be collectively archived is deeply responsive to theories of collective *memory*.

In "Reading the Past Against the Grain: The Shape of Memory Studies," Barbie Zelizer provides a useful definition of collective memory that, in its emphasis on interactivity, conflicted accounting, and identity formation, is germane to an archived WPA history of practice, and to the importance that individual WPAs have in archiving the work of the field through aggregation of experienced-based memories. Zelizer, in distinguishing between individual and collective remembrances, contends that

> Unlike personal memory, which refers to an individual's ability to conserve information, the collective memory comprises recollections of the past that are determined and shaped by the group. By definition, collective memory thereby presumes activities of sharing, discussion, negotiation, and often, contestation. Remembering becomes implicated in a range of other activities having as much to do with identity formation, power and authority, cultural norms, and social interaction as with the simple act of recall. (214)

Noting that while history, and historiography, "at times has assumed a chameleon-like role, taking on some of memory's characteristics" as a privileged (i.e., more trusted) means of recounting the past, Zelizer argues that scholars of memory studies believe "collective memory is both more mobile and mutable than history," especially as new voices are added and narratives modified by additional perspectives, including those motivated by other interests (216). Importantly, Zelizer points out that "Memory studies presume multiple conflicting accounts of the past" (217) in arguing against history as a static narrative. Taking stock of Zelizer's argument allows us to distinguish between simply archiving WPA remembered practices in static, individualized form and archiving these collectively, with opportunity for response, revision, and re-appropriation owing to historical, political, and economic contexts. Understanding Zelizer's theories can help WPAs see that we are more powerful together, in sharing and comparing our recovered histories, and our memorializing of our own programs.

Such a view of memory versus history coincides with a variety of theorists of historiography, as well rhetorical scholars considering the shape and tenor of field histories, such as those in the "Octalog" and "Octalog II" discussions at the 1988 and 1997 CCCC meetings. The concept of history as dynamic and conflicting, and dependent upon multiple voices, is also the core argument for local histories in writing studies being equal to—or perhaps more important than—grand or master field narratives. The surge of "microhistories" in a variety of disciplines, including most recently rhetoric and composition (McComiskey), is also testament to the overlap between Zelizer's arguments and those already embraced within field circles, if not wholly so in those discussing writing program administration. Whereas, for example, the Octalogs go to the very heart of what rhetoric *is* (and how we forward a definition that considers rhetoric's role in historical formations of the discipline, both inside and outside the university as an institution), Zelizer's notion of collective memory even further privileges that process of contesting the *what* toward shaping continued practices, or the *how*.

Further still, Zelizer outlines through extended examples how collective memory may be taxonomized as possessing a number of characteristics. It is processual, unpredictable, partial, atemporal (in that collective memory requires that time becomes a "recreation" reliant upon "nonsequential temporal patterning" [222]), independent of space (even as spaces can validate or represent a particular collective memory), usable, material, and "both particular and universal"—a quality that, of those articulated, is perhaps the most salient in anchoring a discussion of WPA histories and practices as one type of collective memory in need of interactive archiving. This taxonomy maps onto Bruce Gronbeck's distinctions between history and memory, which are contemporary with Zelizer's. For example, Gronbeck reminds us that "History is a bivocal discursive practice, one that is both narrative and argumentative in voice and social understanding" leading to the reality that "multiple rhetorics of the past have been practiced by various groups of advocates. The past can be endlessly argued-over and argued-with. It can itself be a battleground or it can be raided, rebuilt, and perverted for any number of human purposes" (2). This leads Gronbeck to later conclude that "the rhetoric of history is a constructionist activity in the strong sense of that word," wherein revisiting and studying historical acts serves to act as "guidance for present-day problems or concerns" (5). For Gronbeck, the rhetoric of collective memory is "a discourse of absolute identification—an interpretation of then and now wherein the hermeneutic circle spins in exceedingly small rotations" (8).

In both Zelizer and Gronbeck's notations of where history and collective memory diverge from, complement, or fracture our relationship with what we believe to be the past and what could have or did "happen" in that past, we can see relevance to how we might archive WPA historical practice in dialogue with this theoretical paradigm in mind. Both Zelizer and Gronbeck emphasize the polyvocal nature of collective memory—its inability to exist without continual additions, interruptions, and contestations—as well as the limitations of history as a *concept* that is dependent upon staid narratives that are unwilling or unable to conceive of the past as having multiple, competing interpretations. WPA histories are no different in this regard; moreover, they are uniquely dependent upon the ability of those past actors to *speak for themselves* in the telling, as WPAs have long since had their programs' goals and outcomes constructed for them, by administrators and other (for right or wrong) invested faculty or broader publics. To first note that collective memory is *processual* also speaks directly to WPA histories and the need for a robust and dialogic archive of them. Our programs and our decisions are not individual actions, nor are we individual actors. Like the prominent theory of writing instruction itself, we WPAs are dependent upon and defined by *process* as much or more than we are the events that occur throughout that temporal process.

Even more recently, Kendall Phillips has put forward the concept of collective and public memory in practice through work that further illustrates theories by Zelizer and Gronbeck, among others. Phillips outlines the critical importance that collective memory plays in understanding our current rhetorical practices, and even our discipline (here constructed as rhetoric). Such importance is easily translatable to a discussion of collectively archiving writing program administration history, even as this small leap has not yet been made. In his introduction to *Framing Public Memory*, Phillips organizes the collection's entries into two main categories: *the memory of publics* and *the publicness of memory*. In doing so, he aims to distinguish between "the way that memories affect and are effected by various publics" (3) and memories that have "been visible to many, that have appeared in view of others" (6). Each of these categories is rhetorical, as

> the study of memory is largely one of the rhetoric of memories. The ways memories attain meaning, compel others to accept them, and are themselves contested, subverted, and supplanted by other memories are essentially rhetorical. As an art interested in the way symbols are employed to induce cooperation, achieve understanding, contest understanding, and offer dissent, rhetoric is deeply steeped in a concern for public memories. (2–3)

In this excerpt, in arguing that "memories are essentially rhetorical," there is a clear connection to the importance of not just recording what *happens or has happened* in our individual writing programs, but also reckoning with *who* gets to record these happenings, and *how* they are described. This distinction is important, as readers also know, to archival studies; who creates (and maintains) the archive is perhaps the single most important factor in what stories that archive is able to tell. We WPAs are logical curators of our practices, but also susceptible to our own biases. So when we record in isolation—or when we read the recordings and remembrances of others, archived as *practices*—we are frequently ignoring the real issue of bias.[1] Recognizing first that memories are *rhetorical* and second that collective memory is not without bias but is at least a dialogue that allows biases to be challenged and reframed, is critical to seeing WPA work archived *as* a kind of dynamically constructed collective memory, representing a diverse and significant public within our field.[2]

Zelizer's work can serve as a primary theoretical paradigm for constructing a site for WPA collective memory, further refined by Phillips' emphasis on the *public*—an important concept when trying to craft a thousand local histories of WPA work into some larger and cohesive space accessible to not just those WPA contributors themselves, but also to others in rhetoric, composition, and writing studies who want to use such a site to *understand* what is important in that memorialization. But as we think more pragmatically about how a site for WPA collective memory would operate—and quickly ascertain that such a site would need to be born digital, which I will discuss again later—we should also briefly consider how memory can operate in this type of interactive online space.

Ekaterina Haskins' "Between Archive and Participation: Public Memory in a Digital Age" serves as one example of interrogation of the power and validity of memory within a digital archive in order to highlight the affordances and limitations *of* archiving. Her study allows us to further connect theories of memory with the practical implementation of a large-scale archive of WPA history and practice that would require a dynamic interface and dialogic capabilities in order to enable ongoing conversation, sharing, and response. While the *National Census of Writing* is one such existing digital site—as I examine below—it has limited capabilities for dialogue, contestation, and revision. But it can be a starting point for thinking about the scope of a more comprehensive WPA archive of collective memory and practice.[3] We might, for example, heed Haskins' concerns about digital archives possessing qualities of "storage and order" but also "presence and interactivity"—which seem, on the surface, to be complementary. However, as Haskins explains, the unique capabilities of a digital archive puts these two impulses into competition, especially when considering the power of multivocal construction of collective memory within such an archive. Noting that until recently, "public memory was constructed and disseminated for the people, not by the people" (403), Haskins points out that scholars of memory agree that "archival" memory is no longer about "idealized representations and dogmatic iconography," particularly in sites considered commemorative in some way (404). She raises a concern that eventually, "all stories and images will be equally fit to represent and comment on the past" through the egalitarian nature of digital archiving as organized by public memory (405). Haskins' points are noteworthy; for memorials and other sites of commemoration, the need for a historical center that speaks to some kind of "truth" of the event and its participants is valid. When the central purpose of an archive, digital or otherwise, is to gather around a *common* type of remembrance, certainly the notion of "becoming one's own historian" can be problematic (408).

In Haskins' central example, the *September 11 Digital Archive*, this tension is clearly on display. However, that tension—between an "official" narrative and a narrative that is composed of individual actors and smaller remembrances—may in fact be a very productive one for WPA work as archived through principles of collective memory. As Haskins observes, "If in its role as a database of historical materials the Archive seeks to respect the authorial agency of contributors, in the role of a tour guide it strives to educate its audience while respecting its autonomy" (416). Such a balance between agency and pedagogy—in the case of a WPA archive, allowing for individual WPA voices to speak while also making space for other actors reading the archive to *learn*, and make their own judgments about competing narratives—is critical for the kind of dynamic site that I advocate here. We might recall Janine Solberg's argument that "digital tools mediate our discovery and interpretation of historical research subjects and thereby shape the histories that researchers find themselves more or less inclined (or able) to write" as search engines, among other technologies, allow for discoveries and connections that more static archival analysis cannot (Solberg 55). We seem to be in an opportune position to harness the power of archiving technologies in order to not only bring to light individual stories of long-forgotten (or silenced) WPAs and their work, but also to animate a conversation among and between those WPAs, importantly *within* their own lifetimes. I offer that employing the concept of public collective memory gives WPAs a basis for conceptualizing this conversation that heretofore has been relatively untheorized and, perhaps as a result, only partially acted upon, as I will illustrate next.

Remembering Practice: Necessary Limitations

In order to understand why even the best archives of practice assembled across the last eighty or so years are valuable *as* archives, but ultimately inadequate in recreating the collective memory I argue for here, we must distinguish between *institutional* archiving as memory, and the *individual* memory-keeping of the WPA. We must understand *institutional* archiving as what is lodged in official records and university files, often by individuals who are not program stakeholders, and *individual* memory-keeping of the WPA as a situated history, a curation of his or her own memories possibly in conflict with institutional representations. WPAs acting as memory-keepers, despite obvious complications—including those surfaced by Haskins, above—can be the most reliable archivists of the *how* and *why* of program changes, influenced by interactive memories that stem from affective takes on strictures characterizing the program itself. But these keepers must do so collectively in order to paint a full picture of ongoing administrative remembered practice on a national scale.

Public memory-keeping gives WPAs the opportunity to change their programs' historical discourse, rather than simply track it (or have it institutionally tracked *for* them, as in the extant compendiums in circulation, compiled as survey responses), and to contribute to the complicated, affective memories that augment the archive, thus further revealing the intricacies of practice. Better still, when such memory-keeping is cross-institutional, scholars of writing programs can gain a truer notion of inter-institutional relationships, one that understands in-the-moment best practices as responses to ethical representations in dialogue with other local geographies and politics outside that WPA's personal reach. Reviewing studies of the WPA as archivist, we can see that the WPA as memory-keeper is powerful in how institutional and non-institutional readers "remember" and regard the ongoing evolution of writing programs and the teaching of writing. As Shirley Rose and Irwin Weiser have argued, WPAs need to be not only researchers, but also careful archivists of their own programs. Citing Clark A. Elliott, Rose and Weiser note that certain archival "understandings" are relevant to WPAs as they strive to represent their current and past practices: that "a document can have different functions at a different time for different audiences" and that "the form of a text is determined by the conversant's need to express something *within a particular situation*" (280). To work with an archivist is an initial step; to *become* an archivist is the ideal, as doing so gives one "intellectual control" over the archival representation of one's program (280). As that archival work happens, however, it must be put into conversation with theory, as theorizing about writing program administration allows us to "understand the positions and actions of others as motivated by their particular perspectives" and in turn, articulate our own positions in relation to those others (192).

Further exploration of theoretical paradigms for archival work as pertaining to the operations and motivations of groups and organizations indicates that voices in isolation are always beholden to larger institutional interpretations, and counter-memories, that cloud how clearly that voice is ultimately heard, or understood. Organizational theorists such as Charlotte Linde illustrate how an *institution*—which she classifies broadly as "both formal and informal groupings of people and established and recognizable practices" (7) or "any social group that has a continued existence over time, whatever its degree of reification or formal status may be" (8)—both remembers and is the site of multiple, dynamic remembrances. In positing the question, "Do institutions remember?" (10), Linde explains how institutional memory can be represented through two main sources: written documents (databases, archives) and individual stories, or narratives (that are both told and repurposed by others for re-telling). Linde argues that written records are "not produced and preserved only as records of a putatively existent and stable past, but rather are representations of the past which project a probable future use for these records" (12). Importantly,

Linde further observes that "institutions and people within institutions do not mechanically record the past" (14), since every re-presentation of a document, record, or remembrance has as its goal a desired future outcome shaped *by* that record of the past.

Linde's contentions are critical to a theoretical understanding of archiving collective memory for WPAs, as such a significant aspect of writing program administration itself is made up of first, articulating the field's practices *as* a legitimate and second, using those articulations to sustain best practices and create a larger, informed remembrance of the *why* and *how* of writing program administration itself—for both campus and non-campus audiences with a stake in the teaching of writing in postsecondary settings, and with literacy acquisition in higher education more generally. But in our attempts to make these collective, archived articulations thus far, such memories have been necessarily documented with varying success. Part of this may be due to the twin concepts of *integration* and *fragmentation* that field historian David Gold notes are on display in composition's histories writ large, warring with the concomitant need to recognize a "complex, multivocal past" ("Remapping" 17). As Gold asserts, this conflict is usually enacted in one of two paradigms used to construct a history, each of which privileges competing voices differently, in that "Under an epistemological model, contradiction appears schizophrenic; under a values model, it appears inevitable, even necessary" (21).

In the compendiums of practice I will discuss in more detail—Warner Taylor's 1929 article-length survey, a 1993 booklet from the Alliance for Undergraduate Education (Working Group), and the 2015 web-based, interactive *National Census of Writing* (Gladstein and Fralix), also known informally as the WPA census—we have recording but little remembering, speaking but little conversation, and archiving of the present with minimal future intent, at least as explicitly stated or arranged. We can also see the problem of representation in equal form and emphasis—the problem of integrating voices and, by extension, memories while also seeking out a more comprehensive remembrance, à la Gold's epistemological model, above. In these compendiums, we have *production* and *preservation*, but toward a repository of individual memories and histories rather than a more fully realized space for conversation and *re*production (or change) as stemming from a collective archive.

Archiving Practice: And the Survey Says . . .

Certainly, large-scale acts of cross-institutional program remembrances have been a visible part of our field's literature, especially if we open up that category to include English departments writ large. However, these remembrances use notably divergent methods, and individually prioritize different kinds of remembering, secondarily employing a range of actors with varying levels of knowledge of and engagement with the histories and practices themselves. The first such extant archive is William Morton Payne's *English in American Universities, by Professors in the English Departments of Twenty Representative Institutions,* from 1895. One might note, of course, that this is an *English* department survey of practice—owing in large part to the lack of recognition of writing programs as distinct from or even existing within English departments at this time in history. Even Harvard University and its famous "English A" that dominates master narratives of our field was not regarded as part of a "program" so much as a series of courses which, of course, were literary in nature, directed by a series of literature faculty. *English in American Universities* is a collection of short articles written by twenty professors at large state and elite private institutions (including Yale, University of California, Indiana University, Amherst, and Wellesley), as originally published in 1894 in *The Dial,* the prominent nineteenth-century magazine which Payne edited. So in this compendium, we have an artificially constructed "dialogue" of individual perspectives on the present fate and practices of English (literature) departments, rather than a conversation between sites of writing/literature that would re-enact past practice.

The second most comprehensive record of practices, chronologically speaking, belongs to John Wozniak's *English Composition in Eastern Colleges, 1850–1940,* which examines in part the same time period as Payne's surveys, but does so through data review and analysis rather than professor-driven narratives of their own departments, and which was published in 1978. Wozniak's study, while more fully recognizing the position of writing instruction within English departments as signaled by its title (at least on a curricular level), is limited to *only* a study of Eastern colleges—privileging this institutional geography as containing the most significant models for nationwide practices. Wozniak's work, rather than a collection of local narratives, is a summary of secondary findings and conclusions from program documents and artifacts that paints a portrait of how writing was taught, by whom, and within what structures at these colleges and universities between the mid-nineteenth century and the middle of World War II. Wozniak's book is frequently used as a historical guide for scholars investigating early writing "program" practices; however, it may be not entirely accurate, especially given Wozniak's outsider status, and his lack of access to the faculty staffing and directing those programs.

In order to find the first true compendium of something that more closely resembles WPA archived practices, we need to go to an article-length study published between the larger works of Payne and Wozniak. This is Warner Taylor's 1929 "A National Survey of Conditions in Freshman English." Large static scale surveys rely not on local statements of value—which are always affected by ethical concerns for the archive—but instead a representation of *practice* over articulations of identity, or choices. Taylor's 1929 study, first published in the *University of Wisconsin Bureau of Educational Research Bulletin*, is notable in this regard. It would be followed in subsequent decades by multivocalized symposia articulating local practices published in *English Journal, College English,* and *College Composition and Communication*. Yet Warner's is also an aggregation of "present conditions" in numerous programs by one voice, in one moment in time. Situating Taylor's work in this context allows us to see an overall aim for multivocal campus representation via singular curation and aggregation, which in turn blunts voices and data and lacks counter-questioning and interactive response.

Available now as a document circulating mainly to general readerships through John Brereton's inclusion in *Origin of Composition Studies*, "A National Survey" examined the content and staffing of over 300 first-year composition programs across the US. These were public and private, small and large institutions that included single-sex and liberal arts colleges, and elite Eastern seaboard universities. Taylor focused on a variety of metrics, including the prevalence of handbooks, commonalities across other reading assignments, number of students taught per instructor, number of men versus women teaching, frequency of individual conferences, and attention to special populations, such as "subfreshmen," i.e., basic writing students. Taylor provided extensive annotation, while also presenting factual tables charting category responses. Taylor comes to many conclusions that look familiar today: the handbook is "not going anywhere" any time soon; teachers have more pupils than they can reasonably respond to (even with theme-readers present to assist); newer teachers are assigned to the teaching of writing while older, more experienced teachers eschew it; and teaching writing is an inexact science. Taylor uses these program data to make larger generalizations about the state of writing programs, rather than call attention to local or best practices in smaller-grained detail.

As such, typically historians look at the Taylor survey to argue for the decades-long persistence of workload problems in the teaching of writing and to examine the local conditions represented in aggregate in the document itself. Given that his work was published in 1929, it is also an important benchmark in a time when little widespread archival evidence of the work of WPAs existed. But to step back and look at the Taylor survey from the perspective of rhetorical memory, I see different issues in play. Specifically, if Taylor's work emphasizes various problems (and successes) in teaching writing on college campuses, it does so through prescribed questions that themselves assume a set of conditions that are shared by many, and that attempt to categorize the work of WPAs and writing teachers through larger taxonomic logic rather than individual, contextual concerns or subsequent dialogic opportunities.

Taylor received a very high response rate on his survey—over 70%, as compared with, for example, the *National Census of Writing* and its response rate of 42% for four-year colleges and 24% for two-year colleges—but he also created the questions, interpreted the data, and controlled the ensuing dissemination of results; Taylor, like Payne before him, was an ethnographic archivist, if you will. His data hold static in the absence of responses to it, or multivocal augmentations, save the 1930 response from Stith Thompson, published, in *College English,* which largely functions as a summary and celebration of Taylor's work and findings, notably arguing that Taylor's findings are timely, as "Devices already in successful operation elsewhere have been independently invented and the painful process of trial and error needlessly repeated" (78). For Thompson, writing programs (née freshmen writing courses) can only succeed if there is a "continual alertness of directors and teachers in the improvement of instruction and a clear understanding of what others are doing" (80).[4] Thompson's call for knowledge sharing echoes yet today, but only insofar as we *isolate* practice from experience, and further still, from programmatic memories. Taylor's survey allowed other directors to see into the programs they could otherwise never see, but it did not give them similar insight into their counterparts' reasoning or experiences. Taylor's survey is thus a portrait of the *teaching of composition,* but not the *people* behind it; it is disembodied memories of practice that have no human element to allow us to engage them further, or understand their relative nuances.

Similarly, the 1993 Alliance for Undergraduate Education *Profiles of Writing Programs* compendium, a 74-page bound publication produced by a subcommittee on writing programs and assessment, features seventeen, 2-4 page responses from research institutions in the Alliance to a set of boilerplate categories regarding program resources and practices (Working Group). These categories are curriculum, administrative structure, student support, staff, staff development and support, reforms in progress, and "highlight," a category designed to leave room for program administrators to spotlight the hallmark features or accomplishments of their individual programs. Following the program profiles is a narrative interpretation of the program data by the committee itself, in the style of Warner Taylor's previous work.[5]

The goal of collecting these profiles during the 1989–90 academic year, according to the document's preface, was to "enable members of the Alliance as well as other educators to understand in detail the mechanisms for writing instruction that prevail on Alliance campuses" as well as "offer overviews of how Alliance institutions approach specific matters of curriculum, staffing, and support." A further goal was to "obtain reliable and comprehensive information about how writing is taught at the large, research-oriented, public—and influential—universities that compose the Alliance." These were the University of Arizona; University of California, Berkeley; University of California, Los Angeles; University of Florida; University of Illinois at Chicago, University of Illinois at Urbana–Champaign; Indiana University; University of Maryland; University of Michigan, University of Minnesota, University North Carolina at Chapel Hill, the Ohio State University, Penn State University, Rutgers University, University of Texas at Austin, University of Washington, and University of Wisconsin–Madison. As is clear from this list of institutions, the Alliance's document—by virtue of its membership—profiled only a particular *kind* of program, and administrative practice therein—and therefore presented for readers only a limited or partial sense of what a university writing program might look like, or concern itself with, in the late twentieth century.

While the Alliance profiles were constructed in consultation with the committee, and were subject to review and revision prior to publication, as noted in the preface to the document, these are individual portraits of individual institutions, eliciting as an archival record competing visions of what a writing program could or should be. These articulations make the document valuable for benchmarking, for example, current practices against past ones at a particular institution. Examining the response from my institution, the University of Illinois at Urbana–Champaign (UIUC), I can see the contraction since 1992 of both our first-year writing course options and our electives beyond the first year. I can also see that the now-defunct placement examination exempted 18% of all students from the composition requirement, whereas now external national measurements exempt closer to 50%. Finally, I can see the beginnings of our "Composition II" requirement, and a highlighting of the faculty development offerings for writing instructors that continues to be a hallmark of our program. But I do not see the *why* or even the *how*; all I can do is see the *when* versus the *now,* and put that against other program profiles in the booklet—for example, contrasting the in-house placement process at UIUC with the developing high school portfolio program at the University of Michigan. I can see practices memorialized, but not in meaningful relation to one another—and without entry of possibly competing memories (from other program stakeholders, peer institutions, etc.).

The dissemination of non-dialogic yet comparative practices, policies, and philosophies is both a strengthening measure for the discipline's archives, as it tracks our writing programs in moments in time, yet also a cacophonic measure that opens WPAs up for comparative discord, if and when memories collide. In the case of the Alliance's study, no voices and memories *can* collide because they are segregated by location and by the individual WPA's responses in the document; instead, they are in fact *reconciled* in the interpretive section following the profiles, due to the limitations of data aggregation and narrative conclusions following. For example, when discussing basic writing courses and requirements, the conclusion notes that "Expectations in basic writing courses are usually equivalent to those in the regular course, with similar kinds and amounts of writing assigned . . . basic writing courses are also more likely to include some sort of exit review, perhaps a portfolio or in-class essay" (63). While this is technically an accurate description of the data, it tells the reader nothing about what role WPAs took in designing these courses or assessments, nor whether the WPAs themselves stand by these as best practices. The reader has no real direction as to how to read these conditions, or how to use them for local benchmarking.

Thus, while the Alliance document is invaluable for measuring the growth and change of these particular writing programs between 1990 and today, and for seeing many prominent writing programs in one historical moment, it is comparatively useless for understanding how these programs operated in consort—if indeed they did—and whether the answers were representative of the larger historical arc of the programs themselves. Rather, it is a report that stops short of making its data dialogic, or emphasizing which findings are most important to writing program administration in the early 1990s—thereby giving it also limited archival value when set against other individual archival documents bearing similar information that might be found on these individual campuses, ones that could be more fully in dialogue with the larger ecology of the program and institution at that moment in time.

In contrast, Gladstein and Fralix's *National Census of Writing*—an online project that gathers the results of more than two years of painstaking data collection from postsecondary writing programs across the country—provides an updated example of what survey aggregation might do on a more personalized and cross-institutional level, and with the affordances of digital technology. The *Census* offers a broad lens focusing again on the kind of local profiling work started with the Alliance's *Profiles*, yet on a scale far beyond either it or Taylor's, as the web-based survey is designed to detail as well as summarize, aggregate as well as drill down, based on the interactive needs of the user. Despite the fact that the scope and time of the *Census*' research resembles in some ways Taylor's work, it aims to provide more than a singular snapshot of *how* writing programs are run and by whom. Indeed, it is searchable through many different possible filters, and purports to be dynamic, rather than static—a database to which items can be later added and revised. As a result, one might simply argue that to compare Gladstein and Fralix's work to Taylor's is to basically highlight digital archiving as an improvement over print, and to further highlight technology as a panacea to issues in recording collective memory. But to only see this difference is a limited view, recalling Linde's observation that it is "a technological dream that narrative knowledge can somehow be database" (12).

The *Census* is a massive and commendable collective of 680 four-year and 220 two-year institution program profiles, collected via local WPAs' responses to a series of questions about program structure, support, staffing, and enrollments. Pledged as a project that will be repeated for new responses/results every four years, starting in 2017, the *Census* is a robust, online, interactive database that allows for both a mass and an individual vocalization of WPA work, through user choices made when delving into the data. Yet because it focuses on the programs rather than the WPAs themselves—relying on WPA reporting as did the Alliance document, and aggregation of results as in both the Alliance and Taylor's surveys—the *Census* still cannot provide a *dialogic* approach that allows WPAs to collectively affect the *shared* discourse of writing programs. However, it is one model for where such a dialogic initiative might start.

The main page of the *Census* offers three links, in addition to an "About" section, a section for glossary of terms used in the census and notes, and a blog: links to two-year institutional data, four-year institutional data, and program profiles. The sorting of census material into these categories not only calls attention to the unique challenges and responses of community versus four-year colleges—something historically under- (or non-) represented thus far in any of the surveys previously discussed here—but also gives users the choice of going directly to program profiles of responding institutions, with access to specific responses from that particular institution for those who consented. When a user clicks on one of the answers, the larger data emerge to put that local answer in national context. Figure 1 is an example, using Eastern Michigan University.

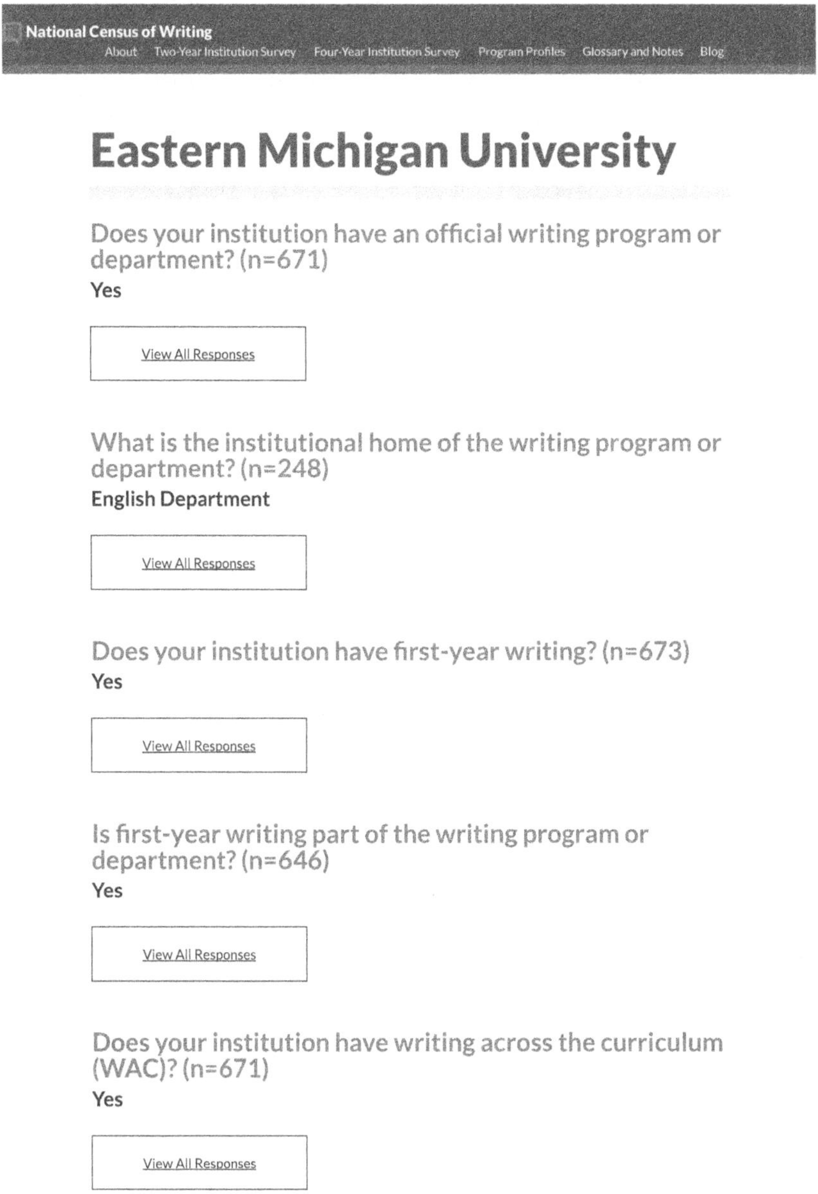

National Census of Writing
About Two-Year Institution Survey Four-Year Institution Survey Program Profiles Glossary and Notes Blog

Eastern Michigan University

Does your institution have an official writing program or department? (n=671)
Yes

[View All Responses]

What is the institutional home of the writing program or department? (n=248)
English Department

[View All Responses]

Does your institution have first-year writing? (n=673)
Yes

[View All Responses]

Is first-year writing part of the writing program or department? (n=646)
Yes

[View All Responses]

Does your institution have writing across the curriculum (WAC)? (n=671)
Yes

[View All Responses]

Figure 1. A screenshot of *National Census on Writing* results for Eastern Michigan University.

Users can also start with a particular question, and see the statistics on aggregate responses. Figure 2 is an example of the results available for the question "Does your Institution have an official writing program or department?" There are a variety of other ways to burrow into this massive amount of data—for example, the question "does your institution have a first-writing requirement" prompts follow-up questions about what that might mean (regarding number of courses, when the courses must be completed, how they are designed). But going beyond the affordances of the technology—which are many—and the overall value and labor of the project itself, which is considerable and commendable, I want to emphasize the rhetorical import such local responses in national context might provide, if able to be put in more direct dialogue with one another, for WPAs wanting to represent their programs in this massive archive. I can point to any number of institutional archives that provide a partial view of how a composition program was structured, or how a particular WPA responded to a set of circumstances in his or her time. But aggregating WPA experiences across institutions, in a public, dialogic context, has additional advantages that we should consider if we are to move forward with seeing WPAs as not only leaders of the present, but conversational, situated voices in the archive directing their aggregated memories toward helping their successors—and stakeholders—who need perspective on the *why* as well as the *how*.

Conclusion: Toward a Multivocal Archive of Remembered Practice

In "The Persistence of Institutional Memory: Genre Uptake and Reform," Dylan Dryer contends that

> WPAs should think carefully about the genres through which their administration is enacted and by which it is conditioned. For if genre conventions organize social relations among students, administrators, and faculty, changes in such conventions can be signals of, and possibly provocations for, changes in social relations. (34)

Dryer's concerns focus on the precedents set through institutional policy-making and document creation, specifically the placement exam at University of Wisconsin–Milwaukee (UWM) and how it led readers to make "assumptions about our students 'needs'" that did not necessarily bear out in practice (38). Dryer observes that in developing this exam process, and using it to determine characteristics and needs of UWM student writers, he and his colleagues "'took up' the genre of the standardized test as our means of institutional reform, but in doing so, we also took up ways of talking and writing about ends that effaced the whole question of students' choice" (42).

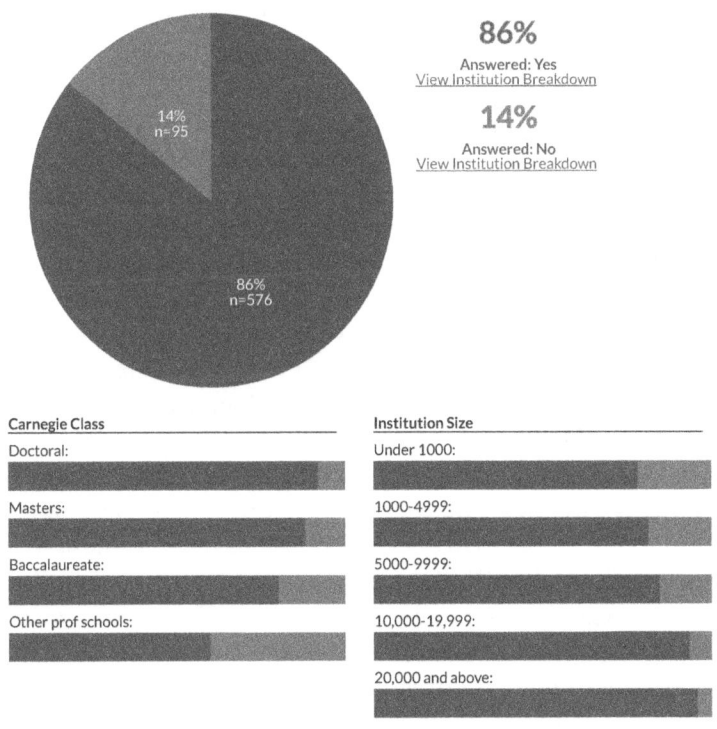

Figure 2. A screenshot of *National Census on Writing* results for the question, "Does your institution have an official writing program or department?"

Dryer's study, while not primarily about archiving practice, is relevant to my own interests in ethically memorializing WPA work in dynamic, public dialogue in two ways. First, Dryer is unusually openly reflective about what he perceives to be a failed practice in WPA work, i.e., the creation and sustainment of a basic writing course that in the longer view may not have fully accounted for students' own perspectives in its design and implementation. But it is Dryer's concern for the institutional memory surrounding this course—beyond the issues of curricular accuracy in the moment—that makes the study notable in a second way. That is, how a local practice will or *should* be remembered by future WPAs and, potentially—I would argue—historians of as well as public stakeholders in that program. Dryer's detailed accounting of his colleagues' practice in this article would seem to guard against misrepresentation of the curricular choices that were made; if anything, the article is far more apology than apologia. But his accounting also illustrates the complex nature of WPA *remembering*, and the stakes in play when memorializing programmatic practice on a local versus national level. For Dryer to argue for thoughtful genre uptake in WPA work, he must also fully account for the work his administrative team set out to do; he must archive this through the publication of the article itself. But in doing so, there are still many voices left unheard—including the WPAs who came before, and their comparative practices; the students who were most affected by the placement exam itself; and, most critically, the WPAs whose work would follow and build upon these findings—or not—at UWM. In addition, invoking the genre of the article *as* archive, as I am here, is ultimately problematic, due to the limitations on its audience, circulation, and productive future reference. We can all, theoretically, publish work *about* our work, but it must be found, read, and heard. And in doing so, it must work in conversation, not isolation.

I employ Dryer's article here neither to call out its articulation of any of its choices, nor to claim that publicizing such choices in this format is positive, negative, or indifferent to the greater WPA good. Rather, I highlight Dryer's local articulation of practice in order to illustrate the larger problem of our absent collective memory as a WPA community, which is notable alongside our privileging of individual memories and recovered individual archives. As a public, we are not as strong as we could be, as we cannot speak truly collectively in narrating our histories as they affect our present. It would be impossible to gather *all* our voices, *all* our memories and histories in one place—I do recognize the logistics of this undertaking, just as I understand the very real limitations of historical work, some of which I've noted here. But what would happen if we scaled up our goals of extra-institutional conversations and remembrances, feeding our memories—affecting and affected by our professional and sometimes personal decisions—into a larger, present conversation that could be dynamic and ongoing, more than just a record of current practices? And how would we do that?

One possible example of how this dialogic memory-keeping of WPA work is already operating on a local scale at the University of New Hampshire (UNH) Connors Writing Center, as articulated by Patty Wilde, Molly Tetreault, and Sarah B. Franco in "Talking Back: Writing Assistants Renegotiate the Public Memory of Writing Centers." At UNH, a desire to both memorialize the marginalization of their writing center and writing centers as a site of under-recognized pedagogical discourse, as well as document the influence of the late Robert Connors in dialogue with current practices stemming from that influence, resulted in an archival project in which

> Assistants offered documents containing individual and collective insights, knowledge, and experiences they hope will promote writing center philosophy while also ensuring their voices are preserved in our Center's past. Instead of a tale of marginalization, assistants' contributions, in concordance with Boquet and Lerner, shift public memory toward the ways writing center work preserves "liberating pedagogies" for both assistants and students. (114)

A primary goal of this work was to have "the assistants crack open the discourses involved in writing center scholarship and enter as practitioners, researchers, and writers" with the hope that "their voices will impact future generations of students, writing center staff, and administrators" (114).

Wilde, Tetreault, and Franco's focus on the voices and memories of assistants not only allowed their team to emphasize actors not typically privileged in the archive; it also gave the staff a greater sense of how memories and experiences intersect and collide, since the assistants also were adding their own experiences to the collective archive (106). Labeling their work a "public memory" and connecting it explicitly to Zelizer's theories, assistants learned methods of archival collection, engaged with various administrative documents that are so often underprivileged *as* archival material outside program curation efforts (memos, emails, training materials). Further, their work allowed them to more fully appreciate and interpret *how* the archival documents worked in the past, and how they might be better employed as programmatic practice in the present; a primary example of this was their analysis of past assistants' training, approaches to conferences, and academic backgrounds (109). As Wilde, Tetreault, and Franco state, "this project offered them the opportunity to consider the ways past, present, and future interact and to engage in cross-temporal conversations with both past and future assistants" (113).

The UNH project also responds to Jane Greer and Laurie Grobman's caution about the *balance* of voices in the archive, which is an important consideration in constructing any representation of a WPA *public* across multiple local and regional contexts. Greer and Grobman assert that "Public discussion creates a shared reality. Yet . . . public memory is imbricated with power relations; therefore, while public memory is ideally a shared enterprise, powerholding groups and individuals exert greater influence in production and maintenance" (13). The UNH writing center project is a robust example of local archival practices that not only keep the center and its historical and present actors in view, but also provides a dialogic experience for future faculty and students interacting with it, and considers the ways in which those voices with less power (peer tutors, for example) lose agency over time in even the most sincere attempts at collective memory.

The UNH project is still *local*, however, and its structure—though dialogic with archives and artifacts—is more time capsule in reality than dynamic dialogue. A digitized, truly public version of this archive would come even closer to the model site I am proposing that the WPA community undertake. Nonetheless, the spirit of this project is responsive to my concerns with keeping memory, history, theory and practice in some kind of continual orbit that makes evident how the WPA community is both public and—in terms of institutional mandates regarding testing, literacy, and nationwide standards—a situated *counterpublic* of many authoritative and valuable voices that act not in isolation, but in response to those who have come before, guiding those who will follow. Such a trajectory, documented in a national rather than global way, is critical, as even though WPA work can be for "life" or simply a transitory moment in a career, the archiving of that position, particularly when done so toward an aggregation of what writing "is" or what writing programs "are," is fraught with positional complications rarely represented in singular, static utterances, or larger-scale, institution-centered repositories of policies and practices.

In creating a dialogic archive of WPA collective memory alongside existing data and historical "fact," a critical question arises: Why has this kind of project not been undertaken before? Why, as the closest model to the one I am proposing, have the creators of the *National Census of Writing* had such difficulty mounting their project, significantly in terms of gathering survey data and ongoing contributors from programs across the country? One immediate answer would be that such work is inherently *not valued* in typical paradigms of institutional merit. While creating and maintaining a database such as the one I'm proposing would be immensely useful as a "service" project for the profession (and likely for smaller subgroups, such as regional WPA associations that wish to, perhaps, subarchive their own regional remembered histories for dialogic purposes), it would be likely unrewarded by tenure and promotion committees. I am reminded of the conversation I had with a colleague about who might next oversee the *CompPile* database that Rich Haswell and others have so expertly steered and maintained in these past decades. I responded that it would need to be someone very senior who not only had the knowledge of the field and ability to find new information to include/update, but who also had the time, institutional space, and institutional rank—i.e., serving as a full professor who was free to pursue projects outside the spectre of tenure and promotion requirements—to devote to the project. And that is a difficult combination to find.

A site such as the one I am proposing would operate, potentially, as a kind of enhanced *CompPile*, one that is built to converse and question and remember rather than just digitize and share. But it falls into the same category in terms of value to one's institutional and professional profile and tenure/promotion case, theoretically. It could uncomfortably straddle the current sparkle and shine of projects in the often ill-defined "digital humanities" and the very unshiny, oft-maligned practical and theoretical world of university administration—an area already shunned and undervalued by our institutional colleagues, as *WPA* readers know. Certainly individual digital projects on pedagogy, history, and theory abound in recent years in the larger field of rhetoric and composition/writing studies, and are supported as research and scholarship by the participants' home institutions; one such recent example is the collection of theoretical perspectives and described projects in the November 2013 special issue of *College English* (guest edited by Jessica Enoch and David Gold). Yet when we think of *larger*-scale digital projects in rhetoric and composition/writing studies, such as the *Digital Archive of Literacy Narratives* (DALN) housed at the Ohio State University, the historical and archival projects surrounding NCTE's centennial in 2011 (both an online digital project and a print project in various forms), the *Digital Rhetoric Collaborative* at the University of Michigan, or even the more grassroots, digitally constructed *Writing Studies Tree* initiated at the City University of New York, we also see significant organizational or institutional backing, and a familiar connection to *scholarship-based* artifacts and conversations. In order to create a site for WPA collective and dialogic memory-keeping, we need both a technical apparatus and a communal buy-in—financially and ideologically speaking—to make the project visible, useful, and intellectual in its design and import. And we need to value archived WPA remembrances and their aggregation *as* scholarship—that which falls into the category of "Program Related Textual Production" according to the CWPA's official statement on the intellectual work of WPAs ("Evaluating").

Thus, on both a practical/materials scale and a conceptual/support scale, we as a WPA community would likely need each of the following in order to make a proposal such as mine a reality, and afford it the recognition of the other field-based projects mentioned above:

- A secure connection to a professional organization, such as CWPA, or another stable institutional site, in order to provide a lasting digital space for construction of this dialogue, as well as reliable access to various contributions, and ongoing maintenance. One model here is the wiki genre, though that format is fairly un-dialogic, allowing for annotation and replacement rather than give-and-take on a particular issue, figure, or fact. Other models are found in open access/digital-born publications or aggregations in our field, though we know that these sites are also highly dependent upon the financial good will of their hosts (see, for example, my previous discussion of *CompPile*). Finally, a partially archival foundation for such a dialogue might be the *Census*, as discussed previously, but further additions to and dialogue with this data would still require an attentive host. Certainly, finding the *place* for collective memory interactions to occur long-term is the first (and I acknowledge, most difficult) step in making it happen.
- A further commitment by WPAs—in a collective sense, if not as particular named curators—to design the space in such a way that it is able to capitalize on the various and often divergent forms of memory-keeping I've noted in this article: surveys, questionnaires, aggregate data analysis, archival analysis, storytelling/oral histories, and testimony. The best space would be able to draw upon *all* of these measures to provide a full picture of how practices of present and past were enabled and limited by particular conditions, voices, and institutional strictures. It would also be mindful of rhetorical memory as represented throughout these forms and genres, and the larger truths of personal and collective bias that inform any kind of memorialization beyond "facts." Finally, it would give participants a variety of ways "in"—from those who want to only deposit artifacts to those who (also) want to annotate the artifacts and views of others—and an argument for undertaking program-related scholarship that can be articulated to institutions as meaningful, research-based work.
- A shared understanding within the WPA community at large that no story, or WPA telling a story, is without consequence, and that no documentation of program practice is unimportant to our larger landscape and public presence. This means striving for access for those who labor outside the known conference and institute circuits

where many of us gather to share our stories; we must encourage participation by those WPAs who are at present not beneficiaries of networking, or more established systems. In doing so, we should not rely solely on the so-called historians of our field (and here I broadly include rhetoric and composition/writing studies scholars as a group) to make meaning of the past as relevant to the various presents we experience on our campuses. We instead should be *actively* making meaning of the comings and goings of our accomplishments (and, importantly, failures, such as in Dryer's study) across campuses. This could dramatically change the way we, as a community, view our "history"—as something that is not static, but actively in dialogue with our present; a fluid time-space continuum, if you will.

Putting our memories and resulting histories into a useable collective space, and conversation, backed by thoughtful consideration of theories of rhetorical memory, is a tall order, but one which I have aimed to articulate and outline here as an initial call to action. The ethical presence of writing program administrators, and their valuation by those both inside and outside the field—especially those stakeholders who affect WPA work from sometimes great distances—is dependent upon our larger consideration of collective memory toward a stronger professional public.

Notes

1. To recall Arlette Farge,

    the historian cannot be narrator alone; he must also explain and persuade, providing detailed explanations because he knows that contrary ones can always be advanced. The first illusion that must be cast aside is that of the definitive truthful narrative. A historical narrative is a construction, not one that can be verified on all of its points. (95)

2. For a fascinating complement to Phillips, and other scholars of rhetorical memory, see Bradford Vivian's *Public Forgetting*, in which he argues the following:

    "public memory" is the result of a perpetual rhetorical process with which communities deliberate over how best to interpret the past as a resource for understanding and making decisions in the present. . . . Acts of public forgetting likewise culminate patterns of collective deliberation or contestation over the meaning of the past as it concerns immediate social or political interests. (13)

Vivian sees memory and forgetting as complementary acts, with forgetting having key benefits at times that supersede the value of remembering.

3. See also, for a guide to the considerations and pitfalls of born digital historical projects (which rely in broad strokes on the concept of contested memories), Daniel J. Cohen and Roy Rosenzweig's *Digital History*. For additional theoretical conceptions of public memory as related to histories of the nation-state, see John R. Gillis' collection *Commemorations: The Politics of National Identity*.

4. For a deeper look at Stith Thompson as a WPA, one which illuminates his own response to Taylor's survey, see Jill Terry Rudy's "Building a Career by Directing Composition: Harvard, Professionalism, and Stith Thompson at Indiana University."

5. The *Profiles* publication might be viewed as a smaller version of Haring-Smith et al.'s 1985 *A Guide to Writing Programs: Writing Centers, Peer Tutoring Programs, and Writing-Across-the-Curriculum*, which described programs beyond first-year writing, and with a wider institutional reach studied in greater detail.

Works Cited

Brereton, John C. *The Origins of Composition Studies in the American College, 1875–1925*, U of Pittsburgh P, 1995.

Cohen, Daniel J., and Roy Rosenzweig. *Digital History: A Guide to Gathering, Preserving, and Presenting the Past on the Web*, chnm.gmu.edu/digitalhistory.

Corbett, Edward P. J. "A History of Writing Program Administration." *Learning from the Histories of Rhetoric: Essays in Honor of Winifred Bryan Horner*, edited by Theresa Enos, Southern Illinois UP, 1993, pp. 60–71.

Dryer, Dylan. "The Persistence of Institutional Memory: Genre Uptake and Reform." *WPA: Writing Program Administration*, vol. 31, no. 3, 2008, pp. 32–51.

"Evaluating the Intellectual Work of Writing Program Administrators." CWPA, 1998, wpacouncil.org/positions/intellectualwork.html.

Farge, Arlette. *The Allure of the Archives*. Translated by Thomas Scott-Railton, Yale UP, 2013.

Gillis, John R. *Commemorations: The Politics of National Identity*. Princeton UP, 1996.

Gladstein, Jill, and Brandon Fralix. *National Census of Writing*, writingcensus.swarthmore.edu.

Gold, David. *Rhetoric at the Margins: Revising the History of Writing Instruction in American Colleges, 1873–1947*. Southern Illinois UP, 2008.

—. "Remapping Revisionist Historiography." *College Composition and Communication*, vol. 64, no. 1, 2012, pp. 15–34.

Gold, David, and Catherine L. Hobbs. *Educating the New Southern Woman: Speech, Writing, and Race at the Public Women's Colleges, 1884–1945*. Southern Illinois UP, 2013.

Greer, Jane, and Laurie Grobman. "Introduction: Complicating Conversations: Public Memory Production and Composition and Rhetoric." *Pedagogies of Public Memory: Teaching Writing and Rhetoric of Museums, Archives, and Memorials*, edited by Jane Greer and Laurie Grobman, Routledge, 2016, pp. 1–34.

Gronbeck, Bruce. "The Rhetorics of the Past: History, Argument, and Collective Memory." Greenspun Conference on Rhetorical History: The Recovery of the Historical Critical Practice, University of Nevada, Las Vegas, 1995, clas.uiowa.edu/commstudies/sites/clas.uiowa.edu.commstudies/files/THE RHETORICS OF THE PAST.pdf.

Haring-Smith, Tori, Nathaniel Hawkins, Elizabeth Morrison, Lise Stern, and Robin Tatu. *A Guide to Writing Programs: Writing Centers, Peer Tutoring Programs, and Writing-Across-the-Curriculum.* Scott Foresman, 1985.

Haskins, Ekaterina. "Between Archive and Participation: Public Memory in a Digital Age." *Rhetoric Society Quarterly*, vol. 37, no. 4, 2007, pp. 401–22.

Henze, Brent, Jack Selzer, and Wendy Sharer. *1977: A Cultural Moment in Composition.* Parlor P, 2008.

Lamos, Steve. *Interests and Opportunities: Race, Racism, and University Writing Instruction in the Post–Civil Rights Era.* U of Pittsburgh P, 2011.

L'Eplattenier, Barbara, and Lisa Mastrangelo, editors. *Historical Studies of Writing Program Administration: Individuals, Communities, and the Formation of a Discipline.* Parlor P, 2004.

Linde, Charlotte. *Working the Past: Narrative and Institutional Memory.* Oxford UP, 2008.

McComiskey, Bruce, editor. *Microhistories of Composition.* Utah State UP, 2016.

Miller, Susan. *Textual Carnivals: The Politics of Composition.* Southern Illinois UP, 1991.

"Octalog: The Politics of Historiography." *Rhetoric Review*, vol. 7, no. 1, 1988, pp. 5–49.

"Octalog II: The (Continuing) Politics of Historiography." *Rhetoric Review*, vol. 16, no. 1, 1997, pp. 22–44.

Ostergaard, Lori, and Henrietta Rix Wood, editors. *In the Archives of Composition: Writing and Rhetoric in High Schools and Normal Schools.* U of Pittsburgh P, 2015.

Payne, William Morton, editor. *English in American Universities, by Professors in the English Departments of Twenty Representative Institutions.* D. C. Heath, 1895.

Phillips, Kendall R. "Introduction." *Framing Public Memory*, edited by Kendall R. Phillips, U of Alabama P, 2004, pp. 1–16.

Ramsey, Alexis E., Wendy B. Sharer, Barbara L'Eplattenier, Lisa Mastrangelo, editors. *Working in the Archives: Practical Research Methods for Rhetoric and Composition.* Southern Illinois UP, 2010.

Ritter, Kelly. *Before Shaughnessy: Basic Writing at Yale and Harvard, 1920–1960.* NCTE, 2009.

—. *To Know Her Own History: Writing at the Woman's College, 1943–1963.* U of Pittsburgh P, 2012.

Roberts, Charles W. "A Course for Training Rhetoric Teachers at the University of Illinois." *College Composition and Communication*, vol. 6, no. 4, 1955, pp. 190–94.

Rose, Shirley K. "What Is a Writing Program History?" *A Rhetoric for Writing Program Administrators*, edited by Rita Malenczyk, Parlor P, 2013, pp. 239–51.

Rose, Shirley K, and Irwin Weiser. "WPA as Researcher and Archivist." *The Writing Program Administrator's Resource: A Guide to Reflection and Practice*, edited by Stuart C. Brown and Theresa Enos, Lawrence Erlbaum, 2002, pp. 275–90.

Rudy, Jill Terry. "Building a Career by Directing Composition: Harvard, Professionalism, and Stith Thompson at Indiana University." L'Eplattenier and Mastrangelo, pp. 71–88.

Skinnell, Ryan. *Conceding Composition: A Crooked History of Composition's Institutional Fortunes*. Utah State UP, 2016.

Solberg, Janine. "Googling the Archive: Digital Tools and the Practice of History." *Advances in the History of Rhetoric*, vol. 15, no. 1, 2012, pp. 53–76.

Soliday, Mary. *The Politics of Remediation: Institutional and Student Needs in Higher Education*. U of Pittsburgh P, 2002.

Taylor, Warner. "A National Survey of Conditions in Freshman English." Brereton, pp. 545–62.

Thompson, Stith. "1930: A National Survey of Freshman English." *College English*, vol. 22, no. 2, 1960, pp. 78–80.

Vivian, Bradford. *Public Forgetting: The Rhetoric and Politics of Beginning Again*. Pennsylvania State UP, 2010.

Weiser, Irwin. "Theorizing Writing Program Theorizing." *Writing Program Administrator as Theorist*, edited by Shirley K Rose and Irwin Weiser, Heinemann, 2002, pp. 183–95.

Wilde, Patty, Molly Tetreault, and Sarah B. Franco. "Talking Back: Writing Assistants Renegotiate the Public Memory of Writing Centers." *Pedagogies of Public Memory: Teaching Writing and Rhetoric of Museums, Archives, and Memorials*, edited by Jane Greer and Laurie Grobman, Routledge, 2016, pp. 105–16.

Working Group on Writing Instruction and Assessment. *Profiles of Writing Programs in the Alliance for Undergraduate Education*. Alliance for Undergraduate Education, 1993.

Wozniak, John Michael. *English Composition in Eastern Colleges, 1850–1940*. UP of America, 1978.

Zelizer, Barbie. "Reading the Past Against the Grain: The Shape of Memory Studies." *Critical Studies in Mass Communication*, vol. 12, no. 2, June 1995, pp. 214–39.

Kelly Ritter is professor of English and writing studies and associate dean of the College of Liberal Arts and Sciences at the University of Illinois at Urbana–Champaign, where she formerly served as director of the Undergraduate Rhetoric Program (2013–17). Her latest book is *Reframing the Subject: Postwar Instructional Film and Class-Conscious Literacies* (University of Pittsburgh Press, 2015). With Melissa Ianetta, she is co-editor of the forthcoming *Landmark Essays in Writing Program Administration* (Routledge, 2018).

Adapting Writing about Writing: Curricular Implications of Cross-Institutional Data from the Writing Transfer Project

Carol Hayes, Ed Jones, Gwen Gorzelsky, and Dana L. Driscoll

ABSTRACT

Writing about writing (WAW), an approach to teaching first-year writing (FYW) that focuses on engaging students in metacognitive reflections about their own writing choices while immersing students in writing studies concepts and literature, offers an approach to teaching FYW that emphasizes transferability: WAW attempts to prepare students to write successfully in the writing contexts they'll encounter after they leave FYW. Not all writing programs can implement a WAW curriculum, however. This article reports on the results of a three-university study, where two universities used writing studies course readings in their writing classes, while the third university—whose local context did not allow implementation of a WAW curriculum—used a theme-based approach to teaching FYW. Our results suggest that some transfer-related factors (including metacognitive reflection on writing choices and attention to audience in particular rhetorical situations) can be taught using a variety of pedagogical approaches, but that students may need explicit, writing studies-based curricula to learn the transfer-focused factor of genre awareness.

INTRODUCTION

In 2007, Douglas Downs and Elizabeth Wardle wrote an article that gave name to a growing area of interest among teachers of writing: the idea that composition has content, and that this content should focus on scholarship and research within writing studies. That name was "writing about writing" (WAW). The concept wasn't new. Scholars have long articulated concerns that first-year writing (FYW), as taught at many U.S. universities, uses a general writing skills instructional approach, when general writing doesn't actually exist: there is only writing embedded in disciplines (Crowley), activity systems (Russell), or discourse communities (Beaufort). Instead of this general, arhetorical, and purportedly pre-disciplinary approach to teaching writing, WAW immerses students in the disciplinary context of writing studies as they read writing scholarship, write in response to the field's scholarly conversations, and reflect on their own writing choices, in an attempt to facilitate writing transfer.

While WAW's focus on writing transfer makes it a compelling approach for first-year writing (FYW), whose purpose is to prepare students for writing in diverse future contexts, not all FYW programs are positioned to adopt it. As Debra Dew acknowledges, FYW instructors trained in English literature may resist teaching writing studies scholarship. Moreover, when part- or full-time faculty, rather than graduate students, teach FYW, writing program administrators attempting to impose a WAW curriculum may be perceived as violating faculty academic freedom.

In programs where a WAW curriculum doesn't fit well, could a pedagogy that adapts some of WAW's transfer factors, but uses non-WAW course materials, convey some of the anticipated benefits of WAW? In other words, could small-scale, WAW-inspired curricular changes in FYW programs produce at least some of the benefits attributed to full WAW curricula?

The Writing Transfer Project, a cross-institutional study of student writing using a mixed-methods design, investigated this question, among others. All participating students wrote reflections designed to promote metacognition regarding their writing, a common WAW practice. In the portion of the study reported here, however, two universities followed WAW curricula, while a third (whose institutional context didn't support a WAW approach) followed theme-based curricula.

Literature Review

What benefits do WAW curricula offer? To date, few empirical studies demonstrate whether such curricula better promote transfer than do other FYW curricula. One attempt at such an investigation, Elizabeth Wardle's two-year study following seven students who had taken a WAW FYW course, could not assess the WAW curriculum's longitudinal effectiveness because students reported either avoiding subsequent courses that required challenging papers or completing writing tasks with skills learned in high school. Kathleen Yancey, Liane Robertson, and Kara Taczak's "Teaching for Transfer" (TFT) curriculum—a FYW curriculum that, like WAW, takes writing studies scholarship as its content via a focus on eleven key terms from this scholarship—does provide qualitative research supporting its impact on writing transfer. In this two-semester, comparative study following seven students across three sections of FYW, two of the three students in the TFT section reported that their FYW course content helped them to think about writing in subsequent contexts. These two students "had a language that facilitated their application and reworking of knowledge and practice from one [writing] site to another" (Yancey, Robertson, and Taczak 99). That language—the eleven key writing studies terms the class emphasized—became a "passport" that guided students across the borders of what Lucille McCarthy called the "strange lands" students face when entering new classroom writing contexts. Yancey, Robertson, and Taczak's empirical study joins other—primarily theoretical—scholarship on writing transfer showing that a writing studies curriculum promotes writing transfer.

Robert Haskell defines educational transfer as "how previous learning influences current and future learning, and how past or current learning is applied or adapted to similar or novel situations" (23). Research on educational transfer suggests that several practices promote successful transfer. David Perkins and Gavriel Salomon's research on "high road" transfer suggests that students need to engage in "deliberate, mindful abstraction" of the skills and principles learned in one context to recognize the usefulness of those skills and adapt them to new contexts, when new contexts differ significantly from the original (22). Writing transfer research, in particular, suggests that such metacognition, often taught via student reflections (Schön; Yancey), can help students both to abstract transferable principles and to undertake forward-reaching learning, by prompting students to anticipate connections to future work (Schwartz, Bransford, and Sears; Nelms and Dively).

While teaching students to abstract the skills or principles useful in future learning is key preparation for writing transfer, once students move from original contexts into new ones, cueing and adaptation become key transfer facilitators. "Cueing"—using prompts that activate prior knowledge—can help students recognize that skills or knowledge learned in earlier contexts might be relevant to new contexts (National Research Council). Such reflections are inherently metacognitive, rather than cognitive, a distinction highlighted by Howard Tinberg in *Naming What We Know*. Taczak extends this distinction to student reflections on writing, defining "cognition" as students naming "*what* they are doing in that particular moment" and "metacognition," as students "considering *why* they made the rhetorical choices they did" (78, emphasis added). In relation to writing transfer, Angela Rounsaville, Rachel Goldberg, and Anis Bawarshi argue that reflections promoting metacognition can help students access prior knowledge, such as writing knowledge learned in high school. Once students recognize that prior knowledge might be usefully mobilized, they must adapt their prior knowledge to meet the new rhetorical demands (Haskell). Students who transfer past writing skills or genre knowledge wholesale, without adaptation, are much less likely to succeed (Reiff and Bawarshi; Robertson, Taczak, and Yancey). Adaptation requires metacognitive attention to the rhetorical demands of new writing contexts. Rebecca Nowacek argues that genre itself can strongly cue for writing transfer, noting, "genre is the exigence for transfer" (28). Rhetorical analysis of a writing situation, then, can both cue writing transfer and guide the adaptations necessary when moving into new contexts.

Recent work on threshold concepts in Linda Adler-Kassner and Elizabeth Wardle's *Naming What We Know* speaks to the importance—and challenges—of teaching genre awareness. In this collection, Charles Bazerman elaborates on the challenge a school setting can pose when attempting to teach students to recognize genre as a social act, as a typified response to a recurrent situation. He notes, "much learning of writing is in school, where stylized and repetitive classroom relations and situations, teacher authority, and student display of competence prevail" (37). In other words, in school settings, the rhetorical situation is so prescribed and circumscribed—the audience is the teacher; the purpose is to display competence; the genre is a form that responds to the "classroom relations and situation"—that it can be difficult for students to see connections between genre conventions, audience, and purpose. Genre thus becomes associated with yet another set of prescribed rules. As a result, Bazerman notes, when students leave school, they often impose academic conventions upon their new work genres, even when those conventions aren't suitable. Without the skills to reflect on and adapt genre knowledge to new contexts, students will continue to struggle when faced with new writing tasks.

WAW curricula promote many of the transfer-related factors reviewed above. WAW courses typically assign reflective writing designed to prompt metacognitive reflection on student writing choices—past, present, and future—by eliciting reflection on prior knowledge, on students' current adaptations of strategies from prior writing contexts, and on the skills or strategies learned in the current assignment that might aid in future writing. Thus WAW can prompt forward-reaching learning. While students' future instructors may not provide explicit cues to activate students' FYW knowledge, FYW instructors can prime students to undertake adaptive transfer in future contexts by emphasizing how each writing task's specific audiences and purposes shape genre.

Given WAW's strong potential to support writing transfer, this article asks whether transfer-related skills and knowledge can be taught using non-WAW content in a FYW course. To answer this question, this article discusses data gathered from three universities.[1] Students at all three universities wrote structured reflections designed to prompt metacognitive reflection on writing choices, creating a common dataset.[2] Two participating universities followed WAW curricula; one used non-writing-studies course materials in theme-based curricula. The non-WAW university's participants comprised two groups: one using a WAW-inspired approach that emphasized rhetorical analysis (analysis of audience, genre, purpose, and context) of the theme-based course readings, as well as the students' own writings and their peers' writings, an approach our team labeled "rhetorical pedagogy"; and one using a non-WAW-approach that did *not* emphasize rhetorical analysis. Having two different participant groups from a single local context allowed us to investigate measurable differences in student reflections, comparing reflections by WAW-inspired, rhetorical pedagogy students with those by non-rhetorical pedagogy students. We hypothesized that students who experienced a rhetorical pedagogy approach would reflect with greater frequency and sophistication on the transfer-related factors connected to rhetorical analysis, such as audience, purpose, and genre.

The rhetorical pedagogy participant group at the non-WAW university was limited to those students required to engage in rhetorical analysis of the course readings *and* the student writing produced in the course (including peer review). We took this approach because, within a WAW curriculum, students experience full immersion in writing studies concepts: they read and discuss writing studies scholarship, write responses to it, and then draft peer reviews of their colleagues' contributions to that scholarship. Thus they engage all semester with writing studies concepts. To match that immersive experience, only those students whose faculty required analysis of the rhetorical situation in a sustained way for *all* writing discussed in the course (course readings and student-produced writing) were included in this participant group.

This article focuses exclusively on student reflections gathered during the first semester of a broader, two-semester writing transfer study, and seeks to find similarities and differences in the frequency and sophistication of the students' reflections regarding factors identified within writing studies as potentially helpful for writing transfer. This article thus cannot speak to whether the differences in the four study groups' reflections correlated with changes in the students' writing over time. Later articles based on data from our broader study will report our findings regarding which factors correlated significantly to gains in writing as students moved from one writing context to another, and which factors presented barriers to such writing transfer.

Methods

Study Sites and Participants

The three universities differed substantially in undergraduate student demographics and average student ACT scores:

- **Wayne State University** is a large Midwestern, public, urban, R1 doctoral research university with an entering first-year student ACT score of 22.8. Its racial demographics include 21.1% African American, 7.7% Asian American, 4.1% Hispanic, 0.4% Native American, 2.9% International, and 53.4% Caucasian ("Fall Enrollment Report" 11).
- **Oakland University** is a large Midwestern, public, suburban, R3 doctoral research university with an entering first-year student ACT score of 23.3 ("Average High School"). Its racial demographics include 10.6% African American, 6.5% Asian-American, 3.6% Hispanic, 1.5% Native American, 1.5% International, and 76.2% Caucasian ("New Student Profile").
- **The George Washington University** is a large Mid-Atlantic, private, urban, R1 doctoral research university, with an entering first-year student ACT score of 29. Its racial demographics include 6.3% African American, 9.9% Asian American, 7.7% Hispanic, 0.2% Native American, 9.5% International, and 58.4% Caucasian ("George Washington University").

While these demographics differ substantially across the universities, the portion of the study reported here measured the impact of instruction in areas where students were likely to be equally unprepared, because high school English classes don't typically focus on rhetorical analysis of audience, purpose, and genre.

Students in five general education writing (GEW) courses taught by participating instructors were invited to participate in the study. Those GEW courses included FYW sections from two universities, a sophomore/junior-level writing course that fulfilled an Intermediate Composition requirement, and a sophomore/junior-level writing course on peer tutoring at another university using a WAW approach. While these courses included first-year students to juniors, all fulfilled GEW requirements. No incentives were used to recruit students for this stage of the study.

To establish a common dataset, researchers collected from participants a shared homework assignment and a series of reflections written in the study's first semester. The homework assignment asked students to reflect on a text they'd composed *before* the semester (usually a piece of high school writing, which they submitted with their reflections). Additionally, students responded to reflective prompts paralleling this homework assignment as they wrote each major paper. These prompts asked about students' writing processes, use of key writing concepts in their writing, any writing challenges encountered, and targeted audience. An end-of-semester reflection asked how students would undertake writing an unfamiliar genre in a future writing context. (See the appendix for the homework and reflective prompts).

The homework assignment was submitted within the first two weeks of the semester to capture students' pre-semester reflections. Responses to the reflective prompts accompanied each major paper; the number of reflections thus varied depending on the number of major papers assigned in a class (ranging between three and five). Because researchers couldn't control the number of major papers and hence the number of accompanying reflections required at the different universities, we only included in our final dataset—the material actually coded—the responses to the homework assignment, the first reflective prompt, and the final reflective prompt. This method captured student reflections at stable intervals across the study sites: within the first two weeks of the semester (the pre-semester reflection on a piece of writing completed before the class began), an early semester reflection that accompanied the first major piece of writing in that course, and an end-of-semester reflection that accompanied the final project.

Table 1
Reflection sets collected and coded from the four different study groups.

Institution and Curricular Approach	Students per study group
Wayne State: WAW	41
Oakland: WAW	32
George Washington: Rare Rhetorical Pedagogy	15
George Washington: Frequent Rhetorical Pedagogy	26
Total	114

At the George Washington University, all instructors teaching FYW during the study's first semester were invited to participate. Eleven of thirty-seven instructors volunteered. To determine which FYW sections would be classified as frequently or rarely engaging in rhetorical pedagogy, researchers conducted a post-semester faculty survey reporting on the frequency with which faculty asked students to analyze audience, genre, purpose, and/or context in three areas: the theme-based course readings, the students' own writing, and their peers' writing. Since these instructors come from a variety of disciplines—not necessarily writing studies—the label of rhetorical pedagogy was not used. Because the IRB agreement for this site's portion of the study promised anonymity to the participating faculty, it was not possible to collect syllabi or conduct classroom visits. That faculty anonymity, however—and the researcher's introduction of the study as examining the faculty's current practices, whatever they might be—meant that there was no pressure on participating faculty to conform to any particular narrative about their classroom practices when filling out the survey.

Three of eleven instructors, teaching a total of eight sections, reported that they "always or almost always" required rhetorical analysis (analysis of audience, genre, purpose, and/or context) of course readings, of students' own writing, and of peers' drafts. Students in these instructors' "frequent" rhetorical pedagogy sections read and wrote about a common theme—e.g., the Holocaust, global warming, or community service projects—but consistently undertook rhetorical analyses.

In contrast, two George Washington instructors, teaching a total of four FYW sections, reported that they rarely required their students to analyze the rhetorical situation of course readings, their own writing, and their peers' writing. Students from these sections constituted the GW-"rare" rhetorical pedagogy group.[3] Data from students whose instructors did not fit definitively in either the "frequent" or "rare" rhetorical pedagogy groups were excluded from this portion of the study.

Coding

In the research project segment reported here, researchers asked whether students taught writing via a WAW curriculum would reflect on transfer-related factors more or less frequently than students taught using theme-based course readings. We also hypothesized that in a comparison of the two participant groups from the George Washington University, students whose instructors frequently engaged in rhetorical pedagogy would reflect on the rhetorical situation (audience, purpose, context) more often.

To answer these questions, researchers developed codes in eight categories to analyze students' reflections: (1) rhetorical knowledge, (2) metacognition, (3) writing knowledge, (4) transfer-focused thinking, (5) dispositions, (6) identity, (7) genre awareness, and (8) use of sources. Each category included multiple codes and subcodes that totaled 98 coding categories.

This article focuses on the codes of "audience" and "genre awareness." To calculate the composite code of "audience"—where students' reflections mentioned addressing an audience in their writing—researchers counted the five related subcodes presented below.

1. Classroom audience invoked (i.e., the teacher or peers in the class)

2. General audience invoked (i.e., "the reader" or "the audience")

3. Specific audience beyond classroom invoked (i.e., "my parents," or "other women in sororities")

4. Audience shapes the writing. This code marked places where students discussed how their awareness of their audience shaped specific aspects of their writing. For example, S22 from Oakland University wrote:

   > The target of my original [paper] was any students in my position who know they wanted to look into a sales career. That audience needed to know what their job would be like, what education they would need, and what skills they would need to be successful in this career field. I made sure I included all of these answers into my essay.

5. Change in perception of audience noted. This code marked a change in student perception of audience over time. For example, S43 from the George Washington University wrote:

   > I feel as though I definitely have a better understanding of what to focus on while writing. I never used to consider my audience while writing before and even though I always thought I was conveying the purpose clearly, I realized I usually wasn't.

In addition to the composite variable of "audience," this article also reports findings regarding the composite variable of "genre awareness," where students discussed genre as not just a formal set of conventions, but rather as a form of writing shaped by particular purposes and/or audiences' needs. To calculate this composite code, researchers counted four subcodes and included both positive and negative weighting of the subcodes to measure the highly variable range of student reflections on genre. An example of each subcode is provided below to clarify the kinds of genre reflections coded:

1. Failure to recognize genre when specifically asked about it (a negative subcode). This code marks student inability to recognize genre, even when directly asked about it in the study's end-of-semester reflection prompt. In their responses, a number of students failed even to recognize genre as part of the question. For example, S75 at the George Washington University wrote:

    > I would approach this situation [writing in a new genre in a new discipline] very similarly to how I approached many of the assigned essays in this . . . course. I would first take a deep breath, and then I would simply begin my research. The revision process would rest high on my priority list as well.

2. Describing genre only in terms of rules/conventions (a negative subcode). This code marks a rule-bound discussion of genre as a series of fixed conventions. For example, S38 at the George Washington University invoked genre conventions as "formats" and "style," but showed no understanding of those conventions' purposes or of audience needs:

    > If I was somehow forced into a biochemistry class and asked to write a research lab report, I would take all of the concepts I learned in this class in terms of different formats of papers and apply it to my biochemistry paper. I would also make sure to research papers of the same style online so I could understand and interpret the format I should be writing in.

3. Recognizing genre as linked to audience or purpose (a positive subcode). This code marks reflections where students move beyond discussing genre purely in terms of conventions to recognizing that different genres serve different audiences and purposes. In a shallow example of this code, S20 at Oakland University wrote: "I was able to easily identify the written genres that I use on a daily basis and to analyze them for what their purposes were."

4. Describing a change in perception of genre over time (a positive subcode). This code marks a change—in the case of our study, that change was always a productive deepening—in the student's

perception of genre over time. For example, S30 from Wayne State University wrote:

> Prior to writing the rhetorical analysis, I thought of genres as simply methods of organizing and formatting a paper; now, I have begun to see the important role each norm plays in creating a persuasive text in a given discourse community. For example, while analyzing the three texts during the rhetorical analysis, I found that footnotes–devices I previously thought were only used to standardize citations –are widely used throughout the I[nternational] R[elations] discourse community to provide contextual support to the discussion.

This student has shifted from discussing genre purely in terms of genre conventions ("organizing and formatting a paper") to discussing those conventions as connected to the discourse community the genre works within, and the purposes and needs of that discourse community (such as the purposes citations serve in International Relations).

To calculate the composite code of "genre awareness," researchers tallied applications of the two positive subcodes (#3 and #4 above), because both signaled an advanced discussion of genre, and subtracted applications of the negative subcodes (#1 and #2 above), because they signaled inadequate or counterproductive discussions of genre. Thus students could have composite scores that were negative.

Coding the reflections required two multi-day sessions: one in summer 2012, with 24 graduate student coders; and one in summer 2013, with 31 graduate student coders. In both summers, we trained coders for at least one full day, based on Matthew Lombard, Jennifer Snyder-Duch, and Cheryl Campanella Bracken's approach, and maintained a minimum intercoder reliability standard of 80% agreement. In summer 2012, due to time and funding limitations, researchers helped code. In 2013, support from two grants funded coding entirely by graduate students. The same core documents—training and norming materials—from summer 2012 were used in summer 2013 to ensure consistency between the two years.

Data Analysis

To determine which statistical calculations to use, we checked the normality of participant groups' data; for the cross-institutional comparisons, the results were outside the range of normal distribution. We thus employed a nonparametric equivalent of analysis of variance (ANOVA)—specifically, the Kruskal-Wallis test—to compare the effects of using or not using a WAW curriculum on student code frequencies across participating universities.

Results

Our research team asked how reflections by students taught WAW curricula would compare with reflections by the two George Washington University groups taught theme-based curricula. Recognizing the different versions of WAW curricula, we also asked whether there were measurable differences in the data from students whose universities taught two different WAW curricula.

Regarding audience awareness, we found that students studying Wayne State's WAW curriculum made statistically significantly fewer mentions of target audiences than did students in the other three groups. A Kruskal-Wallis test indicated that there were statistically significant differences among the four participant groups in relation to the composite code of "audience," $\chi^2(3, N = 114) = 38.34, p < .001$.[4] A follow-up series of nonparametric pairwise tests indicated that the Wayne State study participants made statistically significantly fewer references to target audiences than did the participants in both participant groups from the non-WAW university. Importantly, both of the non-WAW university's "frequent" and "rare" rhetorical pedagogy groups had the highest means for mentions of audience per student among all the universities. There was not a statistically significant difference between the "frequent" and "rare" rhetorical pedagogy groups. Interestingly, Wayne State's students referred to audience statistically significantly fewer times on average than did students from Oakland University, who had also followed a WAW curriculum, which may suggest that not all WAW curricula produce the same effects.

These results indicate that, at least for the three universities in this study, a variety of approaches—from theme-based curricula to WAW curricula—can teach concepts related to audience effectively, when audience is a major focus of the class. (The different groups' approaches to teaching audience will be presented in the Discussion).

However, within our study, student reflections on genre showed serious limitations in the non-WAW curricula. A Kruskal-Wallis test indicated that there were statistically significant differences among the four participant groups in relation to the composite code of genre awareness, $\chi^2(3, N = 114) = 31.75, p < .001$.[5] A follow-up series of nonparametric pairwise tests indicated that Wayne State University's students showed a statistically significantly higher frequency count for genre awareness than did the participants from both of the non-WAW university participant groups. In fact, both of the non-WAW university participant groups showed mean frequency counts in the negative numbers,[6] so while the "frequent" rhetorical pedagogy group did have a statistically significantly higher mean composite score for genre awareness than did the "rare" rhetorical pedagogy group, the overall inability of both of these participant groups to discuss genre in sophisticated ways—or at times even to recognize it—suggests that genre is a complex concept and that students may benefit from reading writing studies materials on genre.

Moreover, when comparing the participant groups from the two WAW universities, the students from Wayne State University—whose WAW curriculum focused heavily on genre—showed statistically significantly higher genre awareness than did the Oakland University students—whose WAW curriculum did not focus on genre—which again suggests that different WAW curricula can produce different effects.

The study's qualitative results show even more clearly students' struggles to understand genre. At the non-WAW university, among the "rare" rhetorical pedagogy students, in whom we expected to (and did) see the least genre awareness, over half (8 out of 15) of the participants utterly failed to recognize the concept of genre, even when directly asked about it. In response to the final reflection prompt that asked how students would approach writing in a new genre in an unfamiliar discipline, the George Washington University participant S165 stated, "I would approach the situation by doing research, then writing up a draft, revising, and then writing the final piece." On the other hand, all of the 41 Wayne State University students recognized genre as a concept when answering this question, a result that seems likely to be related to Wayne State's heavy emphasis on teaching genre in its WAW curriculum.

While all of Wayne State's students recognized genre in their reflections, even at this university a few students struggled to go beyond basic discussions of genre; these students continued to emphasize generic conventions and rules over connections to audience and genre. For instance, Wayne State student S01 wrote:

> Before submitting the R[eflective] A[rgument], I was unfamiliar with genre knowledge and how disciplines acquired their own set of genres. During an in-class-assignment we had to identify genres in another D[iscourse] C[ommunity] outside of our own. I was not able to identify genre knowledge. After revising the rough draft of the RA, I understood the different genres that are in my DC, and how it is important to know the different genres to be a member in my DC.

> To show that I fully understand genre conventions I will use a quote from my final RA. "Genre in business management consist [sic] of memos, complaint letters, reports, business plans, etc."

While this student speaks—at length—about having learned about genre in relation to discourse communities, the student repeatedly describes genres in terms of simply recognizing or knowing them: witness the self-quotation where the student simply lists the different genres associated with business management. This student discusses genre in very basic ways—as typified formats that follow specific conventions that can be learned by novices—but not as conventions shaped by audiences, specific purposes, or goals.

Non-Significant Findings: Metacognition

The statistically significant differences among the three universities' participant groups clustered around audience and genre. Because this article asks whether non-writing-studies curricula can have similar impacts to WAW curricula, however, the lack of statistically significant differences in the students' metacognitive reflections is worth exploring.

The study's metacognitive codes included subcodes that examined how students reflected on prior knowledge; evaluation of writing choices related to audience, purpose, and exigence; and connections between their writing processes and particular writing tasks. Participants from all four groups were coded as engaging in these metacognitive reflections. The lack of statistically significant differences in the code frequency counts in these areas suggests that, at least for the four participant groups in this study, different pedagogical approaches weren't deciding factors in the students' metacognitive reflections.

Discussion

Before interpreting the results presented above, we note the complexity of researching writing instruction and hence our findings' limitations. Many factors can impact a student's knowledge of writing, from broader curricular approaches like those we investigated, to individual instructor effects, to students' different levels of prior knowledge, and more. We do not claim that all evidence in students' reflections was attributable directly—or sometimes perhaps at all—to curricular approaches. Nevertheless, as we show below, it seems likely that the curricular approaches discussed did help shape students' reflections.

Within the limits of our three-university dataset, our findings suggest that a variety of pedagogical approaches—from non-rhetorical, theme-based approaches, to WAW curricula—can successfully teach the rhetorical concept of audience and how to pursue metacognitive reflection. In part, these results surprised us, as we had anticipated that the George Washington University's "rare" rhetorical pedagogy group would discuss audience and purpose less frequently than participants in the "frequent" rhetorical pedagogy group; we had also wondered whether the "frequent" rhetorical pedagogy group's meta-analysis of course readings and student writings would result in more frequent metacognitive reflections (e.g., on prior knowledge, evaluation of writing choices related to audience and exigence, etc.). We did not find such differences.

While the students in the "frequent" rhetorical pedagogy group did recognize genre more frequently, we did not see that result as indicating success, given the fact that both non-WAW participant groups received composite genre scores in the negative numbers. Broadening this analysis of genre awareness to the four participant groups of the study, our data suggest—as we'll discuss below—that genre awareness may require explicit course readings on genre and/or discourse community to enable students to articulate this concept effectively in reflective writing.

The Multiple Curricula of WAW

Our findings suggest that different WAW curricula can produce different impacts. For instance, while both Wayne State and Oakland University followed WAW curricula, Wayne State University's students wrote statistically significantly more frequent and sophisticated reflections on genre, while Oakland University's students reflected on audience with statistically significantly greater frequency.

What types of WAW curricula may have contributed to these results? The Wayne State University program emphasized the concepts of genre and discourse community; genres were introduced to students as forms of communication used to enable discourse community interactions and work. Wayne State University students selected discourse communities to research and explore, investigated those discourse communities by interviewing experts, and then identified and analyzed example texts of particular genres specific to their fields in light of the course readings on discourse communities and genre. Within this teaching context, students often wrote sophisticated genre reflections like the following from Wayne State University student S10:

> Social workers write and read case studies not as a method to determine causation or correlation, but as a method of providing a detailed and oftentimes ongoing record of events . . . This mode of genre

> is extremely useful to social work discourse community for several reasons. As social workers oftentimes do not see their clients more than on a monthly basis, the ongoing case study provides a summary of previous events, which can refresh the memory of the worker in regards to the case. Furthermore, the case study provides the worker with a list of all of the services that have been recommended for the client, and can be used in subsequent visits as a checklist to see what services have been utilized. Lastly, the case study provides those new to the case (other social workers, psychologist, medical professionals, adoptive parents, attorneys or judges) with a detailed recorded history of prior events in the life of the client. The case study genre is particularly interesting in that it employs a specialized style of writing that completely eliminates the writer of the document (the social worker) from the personalized case of the client. The studies are never written in the first person, but rather in the third person omniscient point of view, which takes a panoramic, bird's eye view of the clients, and in describing the overall picture.

Here, the student clearly connects case study genre conventions (lists of recommended services and details from the client's past history) with their purposes and audiences (i.e., providing new audiences, from other social workers to judges, with basic information about the client) within a particular discourse community. While not all students at this university discussed genre's connections to discourse communities with this level of detail, overall this group discussed genre in rich and nuanced ways. Wayne State University's students also read course readings focused on audience, purpose, and exigence, but these factors were discussed more briefly, as aspects of genre, which may have contributed to this participant group not reflecting on audience as frequently as did participant groups whose pedagogical contexts emphasized audience more.

In contrast, the Oakland University FYW program associated theories of genre and teaching genre with the teaching of current-traditional modes, and thus de-emphasized discussions of genre within faculty workshops and in the curricula. Instead, the Oakland University FYW instructors focused course readings and assignments on the rhetorical situation (including audience) and reflective writing. A typical example of student reflections about audience from this university comes from student S14:

> While working on my open-ended project I intended the audience to be for parents of special needs students. I decided to do a web-site because it is easy access for parents while at home. The purpose of my web-site is to help parents whom may not recognize what their

child(ren) are going through. It also helps parents understand how to help their child(ren) at home with different ideas and a great understanding how to keep the child(ren) focused and on task.

This reflection identifies a target audience beyond the classroom (parents of special needs students) and discusses the elements of the project that were shaped by the student's awareness and analysis of that audience's needs, from the genre selected (a website, because it would be easy for parents to access from home), to the materials included (strategies for helping keep children "focused and on task"). This university's curricular attention to audience seems likely to have contributed to the frequency of this participant group's reflections on audience, especially in comparison to Wayne State University.

While both of these universities implemented WAW curricula, their different emphases on audience and genre appear to have contributed to different areas of interest in the students' reflections: one group reflected more often on audience and the other more often and deeply on genre. The implication is that different WAW curricula can have different impacts depending on the writing program's focus and goals.

Genre Awareness

In relation to genre awareness, what were the impacts of the WAW curricula when compared to the George Washington University's theme-based curricula? In the Wayne State curriculum emphasizing genre and discourse community, students reflected more frequently and in more sophisticated ways on genre. Yet even in Wayne State University's genre-rich WAW curriculum, some students continued to struggle to discuss genre as more than forms of writing structured by rigid rules and conventions. Witness the Wayne State student who quoted his or her final assignment to demonstrate that he or she "fully" understood genre: "Genre in business management consist [sic] of memos, complaint letters, reports, business plans, etc." If we view genre as a threshold concept—as argued by scholars in *Naming What We Know*—it becomes easier to see why this concept is so challenging to teach and learn.

In contrast to Wayne State University's students, at the George Washington University, over half of the participants in the group that received little to no explicit instruction in genre—the "rare" rhetorical pedagogy group—failed to recognize genre even when prompted to reflect on it. While the "frequent" group did have a significantly higher mean composite genre score than did the "rare" participant group, both groups' scores were in the negative numbers, indicating that both groups struggled to understand genre. Unfortunately, our research team couldn't conduct follow-up inquiries among the George Washington University–"frequent" rhetorical pedagogy faculty regarding how they taught genre, per the terms of the George Washington University's IRB (which anonymized faculty's participation). What we know is that these faculty required attention to "genre, audience, purpose, and/or context" for almost every course reading and student writing assignment. It may be that these faculty focused less on genre than audience, purpose, or context, and thus a more explicit attention to genre—while still using non-writing-studies-related course readings—could have strengthened student discussions of genre. It may also, however, be that given the complexity of genre as a concept, an explicit writing studies curriculum might be necessary to teach it effectively. How to do so remains an open question requiring further research.

Audience and the Impacts of "Public Writing"

Both of the non-WAW university's participant groups had the highest mean number of references to audience in their reflections, compared to the other two participant groups. Why did these two participant groups refer to audience in similar ways, given that the "rare" rhetorical pedagogy instructors assigned rhetorical analysis infrequently?

The George Washington University's FYW program emphasizes public writing. The program has long held a semesterly student writing event: a two-day conference where multiple student panels give professor–nominated former FYW students the opportunity to present their work to other students, faculty, and librarians. As part of this broader interest in public writing, a number of the study's participating faculty have also arranged student writing opportunities outside the university, from service learning where students write for community organizations; to a partnership with the Holocaust museum where students contribute to ongoing archival work; to open blogs inviting the scientific community to engage with the students in discussions of global warming. Even faculty who don't have students write directly for external audiences generally emphasize the public nature of writing. For instance, one professor asked students to select an academic journal to target while writing their research papers and required in-depth analyses of that journal's conventions, including article length, citation style, and use of subheadings. This writing program's attention to public writing addresses some of the challenges Bazerman highlights regarding teaching genre. School genres can be difficult vehicles for teaching attention to audience and purpose, because their rhetorical situations are so prescribed. Public writing creates contexts where analyzing audience and purpose matters, as witnessed by reflections where students connected the audiences they were targeting and the choices they made as writers. As S51 from the George Washington University wrote,

> In writing this piece, what I found most difficult was determining how to craft it in a way that would earn the respect and attention of the [community organization] leadership. This included presenting the information in an unbiased fashion and figuring out what was most important.

The implication of these findings is that a variety of teaching approaches—from WAW curricula, to rhetorical pedagogy, to public-writing, theme-based curricula—can successfully convey concepts of audience.

Conclusion

This study suggests that you get what you teach: the different WAW curricula followed by Oakland University and Wayne State University appear to have impacted students differently, based on whether course materials emphasized concepts of genre and discourse community (Wayne State University), or the rhetorical concept of audience (Oakland University). Similarly, both of the non-WAW university's participant groups frequently attended to audience, possibly because of that university's focus on public writing. These different curricular emphases seem likely to have contributed to significant differences in which themes predominated in students' reflections.

Similarly, our study required all students to respond to reflective prompts designed to promote metacognition. The lack of statistically significant difference in the metacognition code frequency counts suggests the different pedagogical approaches of the four participant groups didn't impact the frequency of metacognitive reflection, and thus that metacognitive reflections can be embedded in a variety of FYW teaching approaches.

Given the national reality that most first-year writing courses are taught by instructors without explicit training in writing studies, we see this initial study as suggesting that some of the transfer-promoting advantages of WAW curricula, such as the incorporation of metacognitive reflections, *can* be borrowed by alternative curricula, such as theme-based FYW courses. Moreover, a variety of pedagogical approaches—from WAW's attention to audience, to the theme-based courses' attention to "public writing"—can promote the transfer-focused factor of attention to rhetorical situations. However, the theme-based approach produced the least benefit in teaching genre. Perhaps to teach this complex concept, explicit instruction grounded in course texts and/or assignments focused on genre is necessary. Further research is needed. In the meantime, in local university contexts where a WAW curriculum can't be implemented, WPA's and teachers of FYW can borrow at least some of WAW's approaches—its focus on metacognition and attention to rhetorical situations—to better prepare students for writing in new contexts.

Notes

1. The broader Writing Transfer Project includes data from four universities, but because this article focuses on cross-institutional comparisons, the data from one had to be excluded: the small number of participants ($n = 7$) from that university did not allow for comparative quantitative analyses.

2. Demonstrating the messiness inherent in multi-university data collections, two homework assignments were required at two of the study sites, but the third university's students—from the George Washington University—did not complete the first homework assignment. That first homework prompt's questions ultimately focused on areas not reported here, so the omission did not impact these findings.

3. While the majority of students in the GW–"rare" rhetorical pedagogy group "rarely or never" analyzed the rhetorical situation of course readings, one faculty member (whose students contributed 10.5% of the analyzed reflective documents and 25% of the pre- and post-semester, year 1 paper samples) noted *occasionally* having students analyze the rhetorical situation in course readings—but never having students engage in such analysis for their own or their peers' writing.

4. The effect size associated with the differences in audience, as measured by Cramér's V, was .33. Using Cohen's criteria, this coefficient was indicative of a large effect size.

5. The effect size associated with the differences in genre awareness, as measured by Cramér's V, was .30. Using Cohen's criteria, this coefficient was indicative of a large effect size.

6. The GW–"frequent" rhetorical pedagogy group showed a negative mean frequency count for genre awareness ($M = -0.50$, $SD = 0.91$); the GW–"rare" rhetorical pedagogy group's mean frequency for genre was even lower ($M = -1.13$, $SD = 0.64$).

Appendix: Reflective Prompts

Homework Assignment (given within the first two weeks of the semester)

Find a research paper that represents your best writing from high school/last semester. If you have not done a research paper, please find a paper that is based on at least one text.

1. Describe the assignment and course in which you wrote the piece.

2. Why did you choose this piece?

3. What did your teacher do, if anything, to assist you in writing this assignment?

4. Please describe your writing process for this assignment. This may include prewriting, drafting, revising, editing, peer reviews, the research process and interaction with your instructor, writing center, and/or others.

5. Was there something you found difficult to do in writing this piece? Please describe it and how you dealt with this difficulty.

6. What purposes do the sources serve in this piece?

7. What went well when writing this assignment?

8. What knowledge/skills learned from writing this paper do you plan to take into this course?

Paper Reflection (accompanied each major paper submitted)

1. Please describe your writing process for this assignment. This may include prewriting, drafting, revising, editing, peer reviews, the research process, and interaction with your instructor, writing center, and/or others.

2. What key writing concepts, if any, were important factors in how you approached or carried out this writing assignment?

3. Was there something you found difficult to do in writing this piece? If so, please describe it and how you dealt with this difficulty. If you didn't find the writing task difficult, why was this piece easy for you to write?

4. When shaping this project, what audience—other than the teacher—were you targeting, if any? What values and/or needs did that audience have? How did you shape your writing to target that audience? What purpose did you hope to achieve in targeting this audience?

5. Did you "frame," contextualize, or contribute to a conversation in some way? If so, how did you do so?

6. What knowledge/skills can you take with you to future writing projects?

7. What purposes do the sources serve in this piece?

Final Reflection (NOTE: the final reflection—collected with the final major paper—included the "Paper Reflection" questions presented above and ended with the two questions below.)

1. Describe your level of confidence in your writing when you entered this class as compared to now.

2. Imagine that you are in an upper-division course in a field different than your own (for instance, you might be an education major taking a biochemistry course) where you are asked to write in a genre that you have not worked in before. How would you approach this situation?

Works Cited

Adler-Kassner, Linda, and Elizabeth Wardle, editors. *Naming What We Know: Threshold Concepts of Writing Studies*. Utah State UP, 2015.

"Average High School GPA and ACT Score." Oakland University Office of Institutional Research and Assessment, 2013, oakland.edu/?id=9678&sid=250.

Bazerman, Charles. "Writing Speaks to Situations through Recognizable Forms." Adler-Kassner and Wardle, pp. 35–37.

Beaufort, Anne. *College Writing and Beyond: A New Framework for University Writing Instruction*. Utah State UP, 2007.

Crowley, Sharon. "A Personal Essay on Freshman English." *PRE/TEXT*, vol. 12, 1991, pp. 156–76.

Dew, Debra F. "Language Matters: Rhetoric and Writing I as Content Course." *WPA: Writing Program Administration*, vol. 26, no. 3, 2003, pp. 87–104.

Downs, Douglas and Elizabeth Wardle. "Teaching about Writing, Righting Misconceptions: (Re)Envisioning 'First-Year Composition' as 'Introduction to Writing Studies.'" *College Composition and Communication*, vol. 58, no. 4, 2007, pp. 552–84.

"Fall Enrollment Report 2013." Wayne State University Office of Budget, Planning, and Analysis, October 2013.

"George Washington University Undergraduate Fact Sheet." The George Washington University Office of Institutional Research and Planning, fall 2014.

Haskell, Robert E. *Transfer of Learning: Cognition, Instruction, and Reasoning*. Academic P, 2000.

Lombard, Matthew, Jennifer Snyder-Duch, and Cheryl Campanella Bracken. "Content Analysis in Mass Communication: Assessment and Reporting of

Intercoder Reliability." *Human Communication Research*, vol. 28, no.4, 2002, pp. 587–604.

McCarthy, Lucille P. "A Stranger in Strange Lands: A College Student Writing across the Curriculum." *Research in Teaching English*, vol. 21, no. 3, 1987, pp. 233–65.

National Research Council. *How People Learn: Brain, Mind, Experience, and School*. National Academies P, 2000.

Nelms, Gerald, and Rhonda Leathers Dively. "Perceived Roadblocks to Transferring Knowledge from First-Year Composition to Writing-Intensive Major Courses: A Pilot Study." *WPA: Writing Program Adminstration*, vol. 31, nos. 1-2, 2007, pp. 214–39.

"New Student Profile: Fall 2013." Oakland University Office of Institutional Research and Assessment, 2013, oakland.edu/?id=9638&sid=250.

Nowacek, Rebecca S. *Agents of Integration: Understanding Transfer as a Rhetorical Act*. Southern Illinois UP, 2011.

Perkins, David N., and Gavriel Salomon. "Are Cognitive Skills Context-Bound?" *Educational Researcher*, vol. 18, no. 1, 1989, pp. 16–25.

Reiff, Mary Jo, and Anis Bawarshi. "Tracing Discursive Resources: How Students Use Prior Genre Knowledge to Negotiate New Writing Contexts in First-Year Composition." *Written Communication*, vol. 28, no. 3, 2011, pp. 312–37.

Robertson, Liane, Kara Taczak, and Kathleen B. Yancey. "Notes Toward a Theory of Prior Knowledge and Its Role in College Composers' Transfer of Knowledge and Practice." *Composition Forum*, vol. 26, 2012, compositionforum.com/issue/26/prior-knowledge-transfer.php.

Rounsaville, Angela, Rachel Goldberg, and Anis Bawarshi. "From Incomes to Outcomes: FYW Students' Prior Genre Knowledge, Metacognition, and the Question of Transfer." *WPA: Writing Program Administration*, vol. 32, nos. 1-2, 2008, pp. 97–112.

Russell, David. "Activity Theory and Its Implications for Writing Instruction." *Reconceiving Writing, Rethinking Writing Instruction*, edited by Joseph Petraglia, Lawrence Erlbaum, 1995, pp. 51–77.

Schön, Donald A. *Educating the Reflective Practitioner: Toward a New Design for Teaching and Learning in the Professions*. Jossey-Bass, 1987.

Schwartz, Daniel L., John D. Bransford, and David Sears. "Efficiency and Innovation in Transfer." *Transfer of Learning: From a Modern Multidisciplinary Perspective*, edited by Jose P. Mestre, Information Age Publishing, 2006, pp. 1–52.

Taczak, Kara. "Reflection Is Critical For Writers' Development." Adler-Kassner and Wardle, pp. 78–79.

Tinberg, Howard. "Metacognition Is Not Cognition." Adler-Kassner and Wardle, pp. 75–77.

Wardle, Elizabeth. "Understanding 'Transfer' from FYC: Preliminary Results from a Longitudinal Study." *WPA: Writing Program Administration*, vol. 31, nos. 1-2, 2007, pp. 65–85.

Yancey, Kathleen B. *Reflection in the Writing Classroom*. Utah State UP, 1998.

Yancey, Kathleen B., Liane Robertson, and Kara Taczak. *Writing across Contexts: Transfer, Composition, and Sites of Writing*. Utah State UP, 2014.

Acknowledgments

We wish to thank the Spencer Foundation and the National Council of Teachers of English for their generous support of the Writing Transfer Project.

Carol Hayes is assistant professor of writing at the George Washington University, where she teaches in the University Writing Program and coordinates assessment. She has served in several administrative positions, including directing first-year writing and directing the writing center. Her research within writing studies focuses on writing transfer, writing development and instruction, public writing, and genre awareness. Her work has appeared in *Composition Forum* and several edited collections.

Ed Jones directs the basic writing program and coordinates assessment in the Department of English at Seton Hall University. His areas of scholarly interest are knowledge transfer, the effect of race and class on self-beliefs and writing achievement, and issues related to administering a writing program. He has published in *WPA: Writing Program Administration*, *Teaching in the Two-Year College*, and *Contemporary Educational Psychology*, as well as contributed to *Machine Scoring of Student Essays*.

Gwen Gorzelsky is executive director of The Institute for Learning and Teaching (TILT) and professor of English at Colorado State University. Her research interests include writing development and writing instruction, learning transfer, metacognition, and literacy learning, particularly uses of literacy for personal and social change. She has published articles in *College Composition and Communication*, *College English*, *Reflections*, *JAC*, *Journal of the Assembly for Expanded Perspectives on Learning*, and other venues.

Dana L. Driscoll is associate professor of English at Indiana University of Pennsylvania, where she teaches in the composition and TESOL doctoral program. Her scholarly interests include writing centers, writing transfer and writerly development, RAD research methodologies, writing across the curriculum, and writing assessment. Her work has appeared in journals such as *WPA: Writing Program Administration*, *Assessing Writing*, *Computers and Composition*, *Composition Forum*, *Writing Center Journal*, and *Teaching and Learning Inquiry*. Her co-authored work won the International Writing Center Association's 2012 Outstanding Article of the Year Award.

Preparing Graduate Students for the Field: A Graduate Student Praxis Heuristic for WPA Professionalization and Institutional Politics

Ashton Foley-Schramm, Bridget Fullerton, Eileen M. James, and Jenna Morton-Aiken

Abstract

This article joins recent scholarly conversations about professionalization practices for graduate students, particularly those preparing for potential careers in WPA work, who are involved in institution-wide initiatives. We argue such experiences are highly beneficial, but can be uncomfortable and challenging if graduate students are unaware of potential obstacles to their contributions, such as embedded institutional cultural restraints, and are then unprepared for tensions likely to arise when they engage as facilitators in WPA-like work. In response, we developed the "Graduate Student Praxis Heuristic," which asks the "project leader" (mentor/WPA), to engage with three areas: (1) establishing project exigence; (2) engaging praxis; and (3) evaluating process. Specific questions within each section are designed to prompt ongoing critical reflection and conversation about expectations, strategies, and goals for both project leaders and graduate students in an effort to mitigate potential sources of tensions over the course of the project.

> *gWPAs often find themselves in an admittedly "difficult and liminal position" because they must negotiate their identities as graduate students and administrators without being fully one or the other.*
>
> —Amy Ferdinandt Stolley,
> "Narratives, Administrative Identity, and
> the Early Career WPA" (29n1)

For graduate students preparing to enter the job market, the opportunity to gain practical experience resulting in publication is certainly an enticing prospect. Most would jump at such an opportunity, as four of us did when offered the chance to facilitate the development of a university-wide writing rubric with an established Writing and Rhetoric faculty member. While the project indeed enabled us to achieve these goals, it also provided us with unexpected lessons about the complexities of writing program administration–like work, what Roxanne Mountford describes as the "institutional politics of this very difficult job" (42). After the project ended, we began drafting this article in an attempt to unpack some of that complexity. In doing so, we found our way to the scholarly conversation about the benefits and challenges of WPA/g(raduate)WPA/WPA-like work, and realized that though our experiences were unique to our specific circumstances, accounts and analyses of similar complications were not uncommon in the WPA community.

We offer our narrative to augment those already circulating, positioning ourselves between John Wittman and Mariana Abuan's article on professionalizing graduate students and Amy Ferdinandt Stolley's call for the expansion and inclusion of alternate WPA narratives in composition scholarship. Wittman and Abuan articulate that scholarship aimed at graduate students "focuses more on socializing students to graduate school rather than to life after graduation," while Stolley argues for a model of scholarship that accounts for many voices including those in "the liminal space(s) of administrative positions that fall outside the traditional senior WPA role" (Wittman and Abuan 62; Stolley 18). As graduate students who ended up completing WPA-related work without an institutional mechanisms of any kind—not even, as we realized in retrospect, under an official WPA, which was nonexistent within our department—we occupied perhaps the most liminal of spaces for WPAs. We discuss our experiences in an effort to build on this conversation and to advocate more specifically for intentional dialogue between project leaders (WPAs/mentors) and graduate students. We echo the call that Suellynn Duffey et al. make for rhetoric and composition to engage gWPAs—and, we argue, any graduate student involved in similar WPA-like work—in "a collaborative administrative structure" that is "more ethically responsible to the need . . . to educate graduate students fully about the politics inherent in our field" (84–85).

We offer a heuristic to guide the kinds of conversations that might better equip graduate students to understand the nature of the still very rhetorical situation in which they find themselves throughout this kind of institutional work. We address the need for conversations about professionalization that emerged throughout our experience and name three areas in particular for discussion: (1) establishing project exigence; (2) engaging praxis; and (3) evaluating process. We hope to support WPAs/mentors who are interested in involving graduate students meaningfully in similar projects and who wish to acknowledge, address, and carefully work through the tensions that can arise when graduate students engage in work beyond their departmental homes. Further, we recommend that all participants—which may include populations with varying levels of agency in addition to graduate students—engage with these questions regularly throughout the project or mentoring process.

Our heuristic offers a practical way to prepare graduate students (and others) for the WPA-like work they will engage in during or after graduate school as well as new faculty or university administrators. Though this tool has grown out of our experiences as graduate students and, as such, names graduate students and their mentors as the primary actors in this article, we believe these kinds of questions would also be helpful to a larger population. As Talinn Phillips, Paul Shovlin, and Megan Titus remind us, graduate students only remain graduate students for limited amounts of time and move on to professional positions, while the liminal positions filled by such students remain in the realm of the liminal no matter who is filling them (50). In this way, our heuristic can also be used for others in liminal positions in the university, including but certainly not limited to new faculty, untenured/non-tenure track positions, and mentors of junior faculty. We developed this heuristic for the use that Chris W. Gallagher suggests, as "a method for invention and problem-solving" that is "intended to be generic enough to suggest some typical moves and conventions but flexible enough to accommodate a wide range of local (program) values" (12).

In offering our "Graduate Student Praxis Heuristic" (figure 1), we are advocating for WPAs to partake in what Catherine Latterell describes as a "postmodern ethics of action [that] allows us to conceptualize [WPA] roles for graduate students in ways that are sensitive to shifting dynamics of power" (38). This heuristic is intended to enable more active engagement with inevitable changes in contexts and cultures during the course of a project. We hope that by sharing what we learned from this project, we might enable WPAs/mentors, graduate students, and others to move more effectively and easily through writing assessment projects, institution-wide initiatives, and other collaborative WPA-like work.

THE ASSESSMENT PROJECT

We entered the assessment initiative as graduate students often do—as a direct outgrowth of our coursework. This research emerged from a University of Rhode Island graduate seminar in Writing Assessment and Curriculum Design as a project investigating best practices for developing writing assessment rubrics appropriate to local culture and deployment needs. We were all completing graduate coursework at the time—three concentrating in rhetoric and composition, one in literature—at a land-grant university with a freestanding department of writing and rhetoric. Each of us had professional experience both inside the classroom and outside of academia; however, we had little experience working at the institutional level and no experience with WPA-like initiatives. We completed the seminar in which we read scholarship and studied writing assessment best practices and then brought that knowledge to a WPA-like project led by our professor.

The writing and rhetoric faculty member teaching the course, Libby Miles, had been asked to design and pilot a writing rubric that could be used across disciplines at our university. We drafted the initial rubric in class and continued revisions during a faculty workshop. At the conclusion of the semester, the four of us transitioned into an independent study with the same professor to facilitate the pilot program and finalize the rubric. Throughout the project, we worked with tenured, mixed-discipline faculty who taught general education courses with a strong writing component; the faculty who continued beyond the initial workshop to pilot the rubric were interested in further developing their writing pedagogy. Following the conclusion of the pilot, we analyzed data in the form of artifacts and faculty feedback and ultimately produced a final rubric and supporting documents: a glossary, a list of recommendations for easy course integration, and a number of recommendations for writing support workshops.

In this final stage, our professor began transitioning to a full-time faculty position at another university. Though she met with us briefly, we mostly finished the project on our own. Our now former professor expressed confidence in our work as she remotely submitted the final rubric and supplemental documents to the university assessment office. We later learned that the newly formed general education committee would be using our (formative) rubric to develop their own (summative) version. Without our professor's presence on campus, we were the ones consulted when the general education committee had questions about the rubric, and this new responsibility, both an honor and onus without a faculty member to act on our behalf, challenged everyone involved as it came up against the existing culture of limited graduate student institutional contributions. Our sense of ownership was tested, especially when the new general education writing rubric continued evolving even after our input was no longer solicited. Though the four of us were consulted by our department chair to respond to the initial follow-up questions, her suggestion that the graduate students who helped make the rubric join the general education committee was rejected.

We would ideally end this narrative summary with the conclusion of what happened to or with the rubric, but we are unable to do so. We cannot share what happened in part because we do not know: those conversations happened behind doors closed to us, so any further storytelling would be speculation and hearsay. But some of us are also uncomfortable sharing what we believe happened because some of us will not graduate for another year, and we imagine *WPA* readers will understand and appreciate our desire to minimize the potential pressures on the complex relationships and power dynamics embedded in a graduate student's launch from her program. We are pleased, however, to share our efforts to theorize our experiences with institutional culture and assessment initiatives from our vantage point as graduate students so that others might gain the specialist expertise which has been the biggest takeaway from this endeavor.

Graduate Student Praxis Heuristic

As we have sought out literature to make sense of our experience, we have been heartened to discover that others are engaging in this conversation, both in describing their experiences (Duffey et al.; Edgington and Gallaher; Elder et al.; Latterell; Phillips et al.) and advocating for more professionalization practices for graduate students engaged in or pursuing WPA or WPA-like work (Christoph et al.; Obermark et al.; Stolley). Many of these voices, however, come from student-turned-scholars who have had time to reflect on their experiences and then productively share those experiences with the field as publishing obstacles and timelines limit the potential for graduate students to offer productive feedback or tools in relative real time. We have published the "Graduate Student Praxis Heuristic" described here to contribute to the filling of this gap but we created it so that we might, on a personal-professional level, have an immediate mechanism through which to understand our struggles with power and agency throughout this process.

Our heuristic is built on the three tenets of (1) establishing project exigence; (2) engaging praxis; and (3) evaluating process. It embeds a recursive practice similar to the assessment loop into interactions between mentors and graduate students engaging in all WPA-like work (Rutz and Lauer-Glebov). Such discussions encourage critical, continued reflection in practical ways to ensure that all participants have agency when possible and are aware of the limitations when full agency is not possible. Graduate students working beyond Latterell's prescribed roles (as the liaison or go-between, the administrative assistant, or the co-policymaker) will likely encounter resistance from various stakeholders within the institution and perhaps even from within the department (24). Such resistance will never be pleasant, but it is likely and can be productive with appropriate framing. By engaging with this "Graduate Student Praxis Heuristic," we hope that graduate students can be truly professionalized by their experience and feel more prepared to engage in the whole of the position of writing program administrator than coursework or scholarship alone may have accomplished.

Eve Proper, a scholar of leadership and policy in higher education, has argued that faculty mentors and departments that host graduate programs should develop codes of conduct. She writes:

> The relationships between faculty and students should be important to any scholarly society whose members are drawn from academia, and the relationship with graduate students ought to be of particular interest. This is not only because the relationship is more intense than at the undergraduate level. Graduate students also learn from their mentors how to be the future of the profession . . . Scholarly societies have a vested interest in passing on best ethical practices to the next generation of scholars. (49)

We argue, by extension, that any member of the scholarly society in which a graduate student works and is trained has a vested interest in engaging in ethical mentoring practices, including faculty, department chairs, university administrators, and staff. We have come to see that mentorship and training need to extend beyond the walls of the classroom context with mentors outlining clear expectations of both their own and students' roles in the larger project. While discussions of university politics may be uncomfortable, having these conversations with graduate students will not only help collaborative projects run more smoothly, but will also help students as they later transition into productive, competent faculty or staff members themselves.

The "Graduate Student Praxis Heuristic" is divided into three parts intended to cover the entire temporal scope of any project—from pre-activity to post-completion. The establishing project exigence section offers directives to help establish the background and impetus for the project as well as questions designed to help project leaders and graduate students discuss contributions as understood by both sides. Engaging praxis covers the actual engagement in the project with questions to be considered as the context of the project develops and changes, and evaluating process provides guided reflection to help consider the end result. In the remainder of this article, we offer scholarship, narrative, and discussion to illustrate how we arrived at these particular groupings of questions and to demonstrate how such frank discussions could be generative sites of professionalization.

GRADUATE STUDENT PRAXIS HEURISTIC

Establishing Project Exigence (as appropriate)

- Do the graduate students involved understand the project, departmental and institutional exigencies, goals, and/or desired outcomes for the project?
- Are the graduate students aware of the key stakeholders (faculty, department chairs, program administrators, university officers, etc.) in the project, and what ideological agendas and practical considerations (e.g. budget) drive their involvement?
- What roles, responsibilities, and time commitments are expected of graduate students in the project?
- Are any related professionalization opportunities (e.g. funding, training, publishing) available for graduate students involved in the project?
- What are the various personal and professional identities and skills of the involved students? How will experiences and credentials be acknowledged and utilized?

Engaging Praxis

- How are the goals of the project leader and graduate students in the assessment project being achieved?
- What kinds of institutional structures, power dynamics, and embedded cultures are graduate students experiencing at play in the project? If significant changes to these elements are taking place, and if they are relevant to graduate students, how might they be addressed?
- How might these tensions be gracefully, ethically, and conscientiously handled by graduate students?
- Are professionalization opportunities and activities being offered, implemented, and supported?
- How are student identities and skills being leveraged? Are contributions being acknowledged?

Evaluating Process

- Have goals and/or desired outcomes for the project been met for the project leader and graduate students?
- How well did graduate students perform the functions asked of them? Is further training/mentoring needed in certain areas?
- Do all parties feel they communicated and collaborated effectively at all stages of the project? Are there any methods or tips collaborators have for future teams?

Figure 1. Graduate Student Praxis Heuristic

Establishing Project Exigence: Who, What, and Why

We continue to believe that inviting graduate students to participate in assessment work can have far-reaching benefits for all involved: students gain "real experience" to describe while on the job market, writing faculty and WPAs benefit from the work of many hands, and administrators (hopefully) encounter a stronger product or program resulting from collaborative work. Those undertaking these initiatives, however, and perhaps graduate students in particular, must be cognizant of complexities which accompany such work. Linda Adler-Kassner and Peggy O'Neill write about the challenges of collaborative work in assessment, specifically articulating the need to pay "careful attention to the values and passions of all involved, through a process that provides access to all" (108). Though they are talking specifically about choosing the appropriate means for disseminating the results of an assessment, this call for careful attention highlights the significance of power dynamics for the institutional stakeholders involved in assessment (104–07). Faculty mentors often take this into account when planning institutional projects, but graduate students would benefit from a reminder about the inherently liminal position they hold within the university, particularly if they come (as we did) from a department where their work is valued beyond that of mere apprentices.

We developed the establishing project exigence category in part because, although acknowledging the reach of embedded cultural and power dynamics has become more prevalent in recent WPA scholarship involving graduate students, such scholarship often focuses more on the experiences of the authorized gWPA than on the experiences of those engaged in more marginal or unauthorized WPA roles, like the ones in which we found ourselves. Duffey et al. describe their attempts (as gWPAs) to resist a hierarchical, authoritative approach to leading teaching assistant workshops in their recent 2016 article. Though they encountered difficulties with the approach—self-disclosing that the process was complicated in part by their own anxiety regarding their authority—they found collaborative engagement an effective act of resistance against the entrenched hierarchical culture at work in their university (Duffey et al. 81). This category attempts to confront the conflicts that can accompany labor issues in (g)WPA-type work so that both graduate students and those around them can benefit from the resulting discussions of authority, power, and politics between the discipline, institution, and stakeholder populations.

We would have benefited from the understanding that as practitioners of WPA-like work, and as graduate student practitioners in particular, the tensions that can arise around issues of ownership, authorship, agency, and exigence are far more complicated than even the most illustrative accounts can fully document. For example, when we felt like the rubric had been taken away from us, critical reflection prompted by the questions in the establishing project exigence section could have helped us understand it was never really ours to begin with. We also had not fully appreciated that what might be understood as best practice within our field, as espoused by Neil Pagano et al., would not translate into institutional praxis, and that other stakeholders, ideological agendas, and practical constraints were inextricably linked to the project before we even began our work. The "Graduate Student Praxis Heuristic" is our attempt to provide a framework to encourage dialogue at key stages with the establishing project exigence category functioning primarily as an instrument to appropriately manage expectations.

Engaging Praxis: When Scholarship and Practice Collide

Julie Nelson Christoph et al. describe how, as graduate students involved in aspects of WPA work, they "were expected to lead—but [their] authority often was tempered by issues of gender, institutional position, and experience" (94). We experienced similar tensions related to our efficacy and agency throughout our WPA-like work, that, in in retrospect, could have been mitigated had we devoted time to such issues as well as the development and deployment of the rubric itself. The engaging praxis category was developed to create space for these discussions, hopefully at regular intervals throughout the project, so that these tensions become moments for engagement rather than disillusionment.

We participated in this rubric-building initiative in a number of roles: as students within a composition seminar, a graduate program, and a larger institution; as writing instructors with varying degrees of experience; as representatives of a writing department undergoing its own programmatic metamorphosis and staffing changes; and as first-time qualitative researchers invested in generating a positive culture of assessment at our university. We shifted between and regularly moved beyond Latterell's categories when we acted as writing specialists, assessment and rubric consultants, researchers in the field, workshop facilitators, administrative liaisons, mentees accepting guidance, and scholars engaged in praxis. Much of this work was well received in the earlier stages, though many of our later contributions were not valued, and the situation was further complicated by changes in the administration that had originally engaged our mentor in this project. We designed the engaging praxis questions regarding changes in institutional structures, power dynamics, and embedded cultures to highlight the magnitude of the potential implications of these types of change for the mentor, graduate students, or even the work itself.

Though obvious to most faculty, we were not initially conscious of the ineffectual role that graduate students generally play in institutions. Our voices were valued both within our department and the sheltered conversations of faculty workshops, and we were—quite naively—unprepared when the tone of later dialogues at the institutional level shifted significantly. The faculty who were directly involved in the rubric development project treated us with collegial respect, and we realize now that questions such as those in the engaging praxis category would have helped us to recognize the unique value of those personal-professional relationships to better understand our true position as we moved from our department to the larger institution. As a result, one of our greatest learning moments was recognizing our own liminal status.

We felt the shift to liminal space so keenly because our faculty mentor had supported and respected our work consistently throughout the project. We experienced the effective mentoring that Stolley describes as "interdependent" and not just "expert-apprentice that often silences the mentee" (24). Our faculty mentor's approach allowed us to complete the rubric creation and pilot program with more agency than we could have anticipated, and we encourage all project leaders to carefully consider their roles in order to provide the kind of guidance and mentorship that can lead to the most positive outcome. She operated in a "mentor as guide" role, which Christoph et al. describe as "The mentor who guides [that] does not direct or dictate, but facilitates, shows, and encourages. Rather than administering in a top-down fashion, the mentor-as-guide model suggests a side-by-side relationship" (98). While this person "does lead . . . she leads while also making the journey with those depending on her" (98). Even the interdependent nature of this relationship, however, could not change our intrinsic roles within the university as our mentor often shielded us from the institutional tensions we became aware of only after her departure.

Evaluating Process: The (Self-)Assessment Loop

In reflecting at the time, and particularly in retrospect, we have come to realize the extent to which various cultures and contexts at work, often hidden under the surface, affected the development of this project in ways we did not anticipate. While scholars often situate their own studies in a general sense ("at a midsized, land-grant, research institution," for example), assessment articles and studies—the scholarship we read to prepare for the project—tend not to articulate the contexts working in the background.

We struggled with many transitions throughout this project, but we were ultimately able to benefit from the experience by documenting changes in our positions within the project and our understanding of rubric ownership in the "Navigating Murky Waters" article, which won the 2015 CWPA Graduate Student Writing Award (Foley et al.). We appreciate the many roles we filled over the course of the project because they allowed us to understand agency, power, and influence from a variety of perspectives, but at the time, we often felt adrift in navigating our circumstances. We had prepared for how we might support and encourage faculty from other disciplines as they participated in the creation of a writing rubric, but we had not thought to consult literature about the difficult transition we were making from students to interdisciplinary facilitators. As a result, we developed the final section of the heuristic, evaluating process, to guide reflection after the conclusion of a project to echo the elements examined in the first two categories with the benefit of experience and hindsight and to help all involved be better prepared for those factors in their next undertaking.

While reflecting on this project, Eric Turley and Chris Gallagher's law of distal diminishment resonated with us for a variety of reasons, especially when we felt our own agency and influence shrinking as we moved further from the origins of our involvement with the project. Turley and Gallagher maintain that "any educational tool becomes less instructionally useful—and more potentially damaging to educational integrity—the farther away from the classroom it originates or travels" (88). In applying this to our experience, the further away the tool traveled from the context of our classroom or initial faculty discussions, the less positive the culture of assessment surrounding it became. The resulting tensions with power and identity were by no means unique to our situation, but we were, nonetheless, unprepared for this kind of professional challenge and growth. Our hope is to provide critical awareness through open dialogue and contextual awareness to, at the very least, make students aware of the dynamics into which they are entering and have realistic expectations about limitations of their agency in all resulting interactions, but this awareness is not limited to a single encounter. This article has named mentors and graduate students specifically, but it applies to any circumstances in which an individual attempts to effect change in an institutional ecology.

We focus on graduate students most specifically because although Phillips, Shovlin, and Titus's assertion that "Negotiating power successfully among upper administrators while still categorized as a student is a Herculean task" rings true for many graduate students in our position, we suspect it holds true for a variety of other position within higher education as well (53). Both self-assessment as well as summative external assessment, as we know, help foster growth and learning, ultimately solidifying the professionalization experience for the graduate students. The recap and reflection provided in the evaluating process section of our heuristic will hopefully serve the students as they continue through their program and eventually transition into faculty, staff, administrative, or other positions—like the WPA—they may hold in the future.

Conclusion

While we recognize the discomfort that may come from having frank discussions with graduate students, we hope that this heuristic offers an impartial way to at least open these conversations. Working with a common set of questions can help build a base level of shared information that may help all parties when navigating institutional issues that will likely arise. If this tool were to become an established part of researchers' and mentors' repertoire when involving graduate students in projects beyond the classroom, the field as a whole would benefit from having more informed, self-reflective professionals entering its ranks.

The overwhelming call for attention to the professionalization of graduate students, by Cristyn L. Elder, Megan Schoen, and Ryan Skinnell and others previously mentioned, has helped us locate ourselves within an ongoing conversation while also helping us to realize how our experience differed from the existing narratives of so many others engaged in WPA-like work. While assessment is only one facet of WPA work, we have attempted here to connect our assessment experiences with WPA work and graduate student professionalization in a meaningful way. Much of the scholarship described expressed similar feelings of disillusionment with, or misgivings about, WPA work, particularly with accounts written from the perspective of the liminal (g)WPA. As Elder, Schoen, and Skinnell point out in their 2014 assessment of the systems of training available to graduate students interested in WPA work, "persistent statements of graduate student interest in writing program administration" illustrate that the "narrative about WPA work is changing" (21). Where it was once "often characterized as work foisted upon reluctant rhetoric and composition scholars," many burgeoning scholars look to this work as desirable earlier in their careers (21). Like others, however, they recognize the need "for a more robust system of WPA preparation for these graduate students" who are interested in pursuing writing administration work (13).

We pursued this opportunity for a variety of reasons and benefited greatly, but we ultimately hope to contribute to the field with the "Graduate Student Praxis Heuristic" in order to make the process more transparent for those who may engage in similar work. As Stolley suggests, "if we consider only how we are victimized by these situations, we miss an opportunity to theorize, organize, and problem solve to build a system that doesn't create victims of those with less power than we" (28). While we do not count ourselves in the "victim" category, the process was confusing and uncomfortable at points. We recognize that departmental and university service are crucial elements of the socialization and professionalization of all those seeking to become full-time faculty or WPAs, and we have developed this heuristic with Stolley's message in mind. We offer this narrative and heuristic not as another example that suggests that graduate student WPA-related work is thankless and difficult, but to continue to further the existing narratives about the kinds of work that can be done with careful planning and open conversation.

Our initial experiences with this project occasionally left us feeling isolated, but our subsequent forays into scholarship helped us understand that these issues are being addressed and discussed in meaningful ways. Our project mentor often talked about the wedge as the simplest tool and most effective means of opening doors, both literally and figuratively. We hope the "Graduate Student Praxis Heuristic" serves as such a tool, propping wide the already open door and productively pushing at those that are closed. Acquiring professional experience is never an easy task, but we firmly believe that scaffolding expectations into initiatives such as these benefits all those involved, especially the graduate students now who will be all the better prepared for their own work as mentors and WPAs in the future. Assessment best practices encourage recursive critical reflection for a good reason: to ensure course corrections are made, praxis is current, and tools remain effective to the goals of this particular assessment cycle. We as a field would do well to incorporate such practice into our own WPA-like work, particularly when involving graduate students, confirming at key stages that mentors and graduate students alike share and understand specifics goals, roles, and strategies so that everyone involved might complete the process with the greatest agency and efficacy available to them within their local circumstances.

Acknowledgments

We would like to express our sincere gratitude to Professor Libby Miles who took a leap of faith in involving us in this institutional initiative. Her teaching, guidance, and encouragement were invaluable throughout the project. Thanks are also due to Professor Nedra Reynolds for supporting our inclusion in this pilot as well as her thoughtful feedback on our first manuscript, and to Professor Shannon Madden for her fresh perspective on this latest revision. We would also like to thank the reviewers and editors of *WPA* for their recommendations and guidance. Finally, we would like to note that the authors are listed alphabetically by last name and have all contributed equally to this article.

Works Cited

Adler-Kassner, Linda, and Peggy O'Neill. *Reframing Writing Assessment to Improve Teaching and Learning*. Utah State UP, 2010.

Christoph, Julie Nelson, Rebecca Schoenike Nowacek, Mary Lou Odom, and Bonnie Smith. "Three Models of Mentorship: Feminist Leadership and the Graduate Student WPA." *Performing Feminism and Administration in Rhetoric and Composition Studies*, edited by Krista Ratcliffe and Rebecca Rickly, Hampton P, 2010, pp. 93–106.

Duffey, Suellynn, Ben Feigert, Vic Mortimer, Jennifer Phegley, and Melinda Turnley. "Conflict, Collaboration, and Authority: Graduate Students and Writing Program Administration." *Rhetoric Review*, vol. 21, no. 1, 2002, pp. 79–87.

Edgington, Anthony, and Robin Gallaher. "Junior Faculty and Graduate Student Administration Issues." *WPA-CompPile Research Bibliographies*, no. 1, Dec. 2009, comppile.org/wpa/bibliographies/Edgington_Gallaher.pdf.

Elder, Cristyn L., Megan Schoen, and Ryan Skinnell. "Strengthening Graduate Student Preparation for WPA Work." *WPA: Writing Program Administration*, vol. 37, no. 2, 2014, pp. 13–35.

Foley, Ashton, Bridget Fullerton, Eileen James, and Jenna Morton-Aiken. "Navigating Murky Waters: Graduate Students in a University-Wide General Education Writing Assessment Initiative." 15 Oct. 2015. Unpublished manuscript.

Gallagher, Chris W. "Assess Locally, Validate Globally: Heuristics for Validating Local Writing Assessments." *WPA: Writing Program Administration*, vol. 34, no. 1, 2010, pp. 10–32.

Latterell, Catherine. "Defining Roles for Graduate Students in Writing Program Administration: Balancing Pragmatic Needs with a Postmodern Ethics of Action." *WPA: Writing Program Administration*, vol. 27, nos. 1–2, 2003, pp. 23–39.

Mountford, Roxanne. "From Labor to Middle Management: Graduate Students in Writing Program Administration." *Rhetoric Review*, vol. 21, no. 1, 2002, pp. 41–53.

Obermark, Lauren, Elizabeth Brewer, and Kay Halasek. "Moving from the One and Done to a Culture of Collaboration: Revising Professional Development for TAs." *WPA: Writing Program Administration*, vol. 39, no. 1, 2015, pp. 32–53.

Pagano, Neil, Stephen A. Bernhardt, Dudley Reynolds, Mark Williams, and Matthew Kilian McCurrie. "An Inter-Institutional Model for College Writing Assessment." *College Composition and Communication*, vol. 60, no. 2, 2008, pp. 285–320.

Phillips, Talinn, Paul Shovlin, and Megan Titus. "Thinking Liminally: Exploring the (com) Promising Positions of the Liminal WPA." *WPA: Writing Program Administration*, vol. 38, no.1, 2014, pp. 42–64.

Proper, Eve. "Toward a Code of Conduct for Graduate Education." *New Directions for Higher Education*, vol. 160, 2012, pp. 49–59.

Rutz, Carol, and Jacqulyn Lauer-Glebov. "Assessment and Innovation: One Darn Thing Leads to Another." *Assessing Writing*, vol. 10, no. 2, 2005, pp. 80–99.

Stolley, Amy Ferdinandt. "Narratives, Administrative Identity, and the Early Career WPA." *WPA: Writing Program Administration*, vol. 39, no. 1, 2015, pp. 18–31.

Turley, Eric D., and Chris W. Gallagher. "On the 'Uses' of Rubrics: Reframing the Great Rubric Debate." *The English Journal*, vol. 97, no. 4, 2008, pp. 87–92.

Wittman, John, and Mariana Abuan. "Socializing Future Professionals Exploring the Matrix of Assessment." *Pedagogy*, vol. 15, no. 1, 2015, pp. 59–70.

Ashton Foley-Schramm is a PhD candidate in English specializing in literature at the University of Rhode Island. Her research focuses on nineteenth-century British literature, especially the novel, and representations of reading. She is currently working on her dissertation entitled "Reading the Reader: Analyzing Depictions of Male Readers in Nineteenth Century Fiction." Ashton has presented at national and local conferences, including the CWPA and the Conference on College Composition and Communication.

Bridget Fullerton is assistant director of writing for the humanities, social sciences and interdisciplinary studies at Bates College. She supports faculty as writers and as mentors of student writers, contributes and assesses WAC programming, and provides mentorship and training for peer educators in the Bates College Academic Resource Commons. Her research interests include student-inclusive assessment, relational and ethical cross-curricular literacy work, and multimodal, embodied and contemplative writing practices.

Eileen M. James is assistant professor of English at the Community College of Rhode Island. Her work appears in *FORUM: Issues about Part-Time and Contingent Faculty* and in the National Association of African American Studies and Affiliates monograph series. She is a PhD candidate in English specializing in writing and rhetoric at the University of Rhode Island.

Jenna Morton-Aiken begins in fall 2018 as assistant professor of humanities at the Massachusetts Maritime Academy. Her research interests include networked archival practice, assessment, and interdisciplinary writing support programs. She teaches undergraduate composition and helped launch SciWrite@URI, an NSF-funded science writing initiative at the University of Rhode Island.

"Everyone Should Have a Plan": A Neoliberal Primer for Writing Program Directors

Nancy Welch

Abstract

While writing programs try to find good solutions to the problems we face, we do so within the conditions and constraints of neoliberalism which systematically casualizes labor, privatizes public services, and reduces social supports within and beyond higher education. Of particular concern for scholars in composition and rhetoric and for writing program directors is how neoliberalism operates rhetorically to train faculty and students to understand problems and seek their solutions in free-market terms. This plenary address offers a primer of neoliberal rhetorics and realities to help writing program directors come to terms with and find more effective and collective ways to resist this "do-more-with-less" political-economic agenda.

Because the conference theme is "Solving Problems Together," Tony Scott and I want to situate the problems facing writing programs in the bigger context of neoliberal political economy. To paraphrase Marx, writing program directors try to find good solutions to the problems we face, but we do not do so in conditions of our own choosing. Our presentations are about critically elaborating the political-economic agenda that has largely shaped the conditions most or all of us find ourselves working within. In a nutshell, to solve problems, we need an elaborated understanding of what the problems and their drivers are. My role is to present a primer of neoliberal rhetorics and realities.

First, definitions. Neoliberalism is what has largely emerged as a global consensus that recurring crises in capital accumulation can be solved and corporate profitability restored through labor casualization, deregulation, reducing or eliminating social supports, and privatizing formerly public institutions and resources, including education, so as to reduce the cost of doing business and create new markets for doing business (the education market, the healthcare market, the student loan market, and so on). June Jordan summed up neoliberalism brilliantly in her Reagan-era "Poem Towards a Final Solution":

> An unidentified reporter then queried the Secretary as to whether this plan could be fairly be translated as take down the trees, tear-up the earth, evacuate the urban poor, and let the people hang, generally speaking. (96)

Neoliberalism isn't only rhetorical: it is materially rooted in persistent economic crises from the 1970s onward. But what I'm especially interested in today is the rhetoric that trains us to see problems and their solutions in free market terms—the role of rhetoric in the social reproduction of neoliberal ideas. For instance, in the 1990s—the era in which the Clinton administration pushed for "managed care" rather than a national "Medicare for All" solution to healthcare coverage—the Northwestern National Life Insurance Company ran a series of advertisements (which you can view at jerryfury.com/northwestern-national-life/) in human resource management magazines. These ads peddled health coverage policies that restrict benefits and shift premium costs from employer to employee. One ad suggests workers are hypochondriacs who, without gatekeeping checks, will run to the doctor "for every little thing" (Fury). Another argues that it is easier to train a dog for a tricycle-riding circus act than to teach employees to use their benefits wisely. For an audience of benefits managers, Northwestern National Life presents employee health insurance use as a problem and chirpily says, "Let's do something about it." The rhetorical work of such ads, of which this series is just one example, was to shift the nation's understanding of healthcare: from what since post–World War II era had been viewed as part of "labor's share" of the wealth workers produce to defining health benefits as a drain, a burdensome tax, or an unappreciated "gift."

Beyond training and disciplining the population to see themselves as consumers in all realms, including healthcare and education, neoliberalism's upward transfer of wealth has been facilitated by directing blame downward: making scapegoats of immigrants or "illegals" who are illogically said both to be lazy and to steal American jobs, chastising black men for a presumed lack of family values, dismissing black and brown kids as "no angel" when shot dead by the police, and faulting working-class homebuyers for accepting the bait of predatory lenders. In a stunning neoliberal sleight of hand, *The Economist* devotes its January 8, 2011 issue to faulting the entire public sector for causing the near collapse of the global finance system and ensuing Great Recession. An editorial cartoon in that issue depicts public-sector workers as a gluttonous woman demanding "fewer hours," "bigger unions," and "better pay" while a tiny business-suited man appears to implore her to restrain her appetite and flames engulf them both. In sum, this issue of *The Economist* celebrates a massive financial crisis that was caused by rapacious private-sector greed as an opportunity to shift the blame onto the public sector. As its January 2011 cover proclaims, this issue declares war on public-sector workers, teachers, and their unions, the first major battle erupting in Wisconsin only a month later.

Neoliberalism depends on the packaging of a world view that includes not only privatizing public resources and dismantling public services but also on privatizing—offloading onto the individual or nuclear family—social needs. And well beyond the financial press, it needs to promote justifications for "letting the people hang." Consider, for instance, an ad from the Department of Homeland Security, which includes the Federal Emergency Management Agency (FEMA), that ran during the summer of 2006 in such upscale magazines as *Food and Wine*. Under the banner "Everyone Should Have a Plan," the ad features a white, middle-class family standing outside their tidy, flag-adorned suburban home. In case of "terrorist attack or other emergency," each family member—even the mannerly white Labrador retriever—has a role. The bread-winning dad will "Fill up the gas tank, drive home [from the office], pack minivan with emergency kit." The apparently stay-at-home mom (presumably in the family's second car) will fetch the kids from school, then return home to ready the family's "overnight bags" and await "official instructions." Every family should have their own (privately funded, self-provisioned) plan, the ad advises, adding, "There's no reason not to."

At first glance, such an ad might seem benign, even banal—just another piece of the neoliberal educational apparatus promoting leave-it-to-the-family solutions for mass public needs. For abundantly provisioned *Food and Wine* elites, such counsel may seem reasonable and wise, a matter of common sense. But consider, too, this additional piece of the ad's historical and rhetorical context: It and similar ads in the campaign ran less than a year after Hurricane Katrina stranded thousands of poor and predominantly black New Orleanians and it ran despite the failure of privatized evacuation plans that resulted in drained gas pumps and clogged highways as Texans tried to flee Hurricane Rita. In this rhetorical context, we can understand the work of the "Everyone should have a plan" ad not as deliberative, concerned with assisting readers in puzzling through how to respond to the next mass shooting or climate disaster but instead as epideictic: ceremonially offloading blame for debacles from Homeland Security and FEMA onto the poor instead. Everyone should have their own privatized plan; no one should expect mass social supports for mass social problems.

The project of the chapters collected in *Composition in the Age of Austerity* (Welch and Scott) is to reveal the connections between this broader articulation of neoliberal realities and rhetorics and the specific conditions and challenges for composition programs in neoliberalized universities—programs that are admonished to come up with their own self-provisioning plans to deliver first-year composition and basic writing, prison literacy programs, the National Writing Project, and more. The urgent question is, of course, what to do. Even though we did not put together *Composition in the Age of Austerity* with the impossible aim of providing solutions to a political-economic consensus that extends well beyond any one college, university, or university administrator, contributors do offer some very good counsel—about coalition-building and solidarity, for instance—and instances of effective resistance—such as the University of Illinois at Chicago faculty strike in 2014 or Quebec's province-wide casserole protests in 2012. To these I want to add a few more.

First, understand that the scarcities we're facing are manufactured. It's not that there isn't money enough but that the money has been funneled elsewhere. At my university, for instance, a decade-long trend of replacing an aging, tenure-track professoriate with contingent faculty has netted the university close to $12 million annually for spending on administrative activities outside the academic mission (Bunsis). The university's budget hasn't gotten smaller; the share for academics is what's gotten smaller. So, understanding where the money comes from and where the money goes really matters. That's something that we can do at my home institution of University of Vermont (UVM) because all faculty—full-time and part-time, tenure-track and non-tenure-track—are unionized. We're able to enlist the help of AAUP in auditing the university's financial records *and* then find ways to provide some counter-rhetorical education for the campus. In one such event, faculty invited students outside the library to spin a "Wheel of Misfortune" and learn about the golden parachutes and secret bonuses claimed by top administrators while staff and lecturers faced cuts. In coming together to plan and stage such an event, faculty step out of an exclusive focus on their programs and internecine competition between departments to—as several contributors in *Composition in the Age of Austerity* likewise advise—seek alliances and build solidarity. In fact, the Wheel of Misfortune emcee was a professor in environmental engineering who was also gravely concerned that first-year composition for engineering students was being stripped of critical inquiry and restless creativity in favor of narrowly instrumental outcomes.

Scholars in composition and rhetoric can also take up as a key research topic how neoliberal rhetoric works and consider what role our curricula can play in teaching students discernment and resistance. I've already touched on the blame-shifts, sleights of hand, and appeals to bootstraps self-reliance. And I've noted *The Economist* as one example of where neoliberalism's architects talk openly and transparently about what they're up to and why. But, as I've written elsewhere (Welch, "*La Langue*"; see also Lecercle), neoliberal rhetoric operates above all through obfuscation: through the fuzzy rhetorical games of *la langue de coton*, or woolen rhetoric. We can, of course, take *la langue de coton* as empty rhetoric—as in this excerpt from *Across the Green*, a regular series of memos distributed by my university's provost:

> We have been careful and purposeful in planning for the changes underway at UVM, with critical input and participation by faculty and staff, but the flywheel is most certainly spinning now. If I can extend this metaphor just a bit more, I would characterize the flywheel at maximum rotational velocity now. We took about three years to get to this point, but we should not expect the rate of change to increase without bound. We are moving at a good pace and are guided by a clear set of goals. The key now is to remain engaged and committed to our shared goals of academic excellence and student success—to keep the flywheel spinning. (Rosowsky)

Yet these kinds of somnambulistic administrative texts that arrive through email or that we hear in Faculty Senate meetings week in and week out *do* effective persuasive work. Most especially, neoliberalism's *langue de coton* aims to persuade an audience that there has already been, usually among vague "stakeholders," a democratic process of consultation and that the present course is one everyone has already agreed on. (See Lecercle for more on the markers of neoliberal discourse.) In the above example, the "flywheel" of university restructuring—that is, the imposition of austerity measures and the promotion of entrepreneurialism—is already spinning and now the task is to keep it going. The memo tells readers that change is already happening, has already been decided upon, and vague "stakeholders" have already been consulted: neoliberalism depends on the presupposition of consensus, usually cast in passive voice. I'll confess that one way I deal with the woolen rhetoric that comes into my email inbox is to cut it and paste it into Helen Sword's "The Writers' Diet Test." But more seriously, I think we need to contend with how vulnerable our own cherished rhetorical ideals and pedagogies make us and our students to these fuzzy claims of consultation, consensus, and neoliberalized civility.

Before I unpack this more, an historical footnote: In summer 2017 I attended a commemoration of the 40th anniversary of the Combahee River

Collective Statement (Frazier et al.), an early articulation of the intersectional understanding that the injustices produced by manifold forms of oppression and class exploitation don't occur on separate planes but simultaneously (Combahee River Collective). With its declaration that "When Black women get free, we all get free" (134), the Combahee River Collective Statement presages the primary assertion of today's Black Lives Matter movement: When black people get free, we all get free. In her remarks for the 40th anniversary panel, Barbara Smith also talked about the events shaping her own political consciousness. The particular event she mentioned that really caught my attention was the 1969 mass student sit-down at the University of Chicago in defense of a sociology professor turned down for tenure shortly after she spoke publicly against the war in Vietnam. Smith was a part of that protest. Her sense of the sit-in's importance and also the problems it revealed with New Left masculinism and middle-class white feminism moved her toward formulating a black and socialist feminist vision.

This moment in Barbara Smith's biography caught my attention because the dean the protest was waged against was eminent rhetorician Wayne Booth. What the students sought to persuade him of was that the sociology professor should be granted tenure and that governance at the University of Chicago should be democratized to include students and residents of the surrounding community. Booth's response: "Well, if there's anything I can do for you short of giving you what you want, please let me know" (Golus). What happened in the end is that Booth oversaw the dismissal—through suspensions and expulsions—of scores of the students for what he saw as a coercive, not a rhetorical, act. (See the introduction to Booth's *Modern Dogma and the Rhetoric of Assent* for his account of the sit-in and its influence on his rhetorical thinking. See also Welch, "Informed," for an extended discussion of Booth's civility rhetoric).

Barbara Smith and Wayne Booth both represent a set of ideas and a history that many of us want to claim for our scholarship and our daily work. Yet they also present two very different positions from which to see the University of Chicago sit-in that was, for both, a defining moment—and two very different articulations of the problem that moment presented. For Barbara Smith, it was one of several consciousness-raising encounters that led her to co-author the Combahee River Collective Statement and lay out the problem of how to build a liberation movement that could take on all interlocking forms of oppression. For Booth, the sit-in was a perplexing refusal of a dean's traditional authority that led him to write *Modern Dogma and the Rhetoric of Assent* and define the problem as the "inability of most protest groups to get themselves heard . . . and [of administrators] to make their responses intelligible" (ix).

In fact, it's because protest groups of the 1960s *did* get themselves heard that universities saw in the student body, faculty, and curriculum the significant democratization that neoliberalism has since rolled back. Student strikes at City College of New York, San Francisco State University, and elsewhere created the conditions for composition as a contemporary discipline. But in *Modern Dogma* and other foundational writing in composition and rhetoric, we have the articulation of ideals that have shaped contemporary composition pedagogies: the ideals of people coming together on a plane of equality to solve problems together not through debate or protest or argument but through cooperation, mediation, fact-based discursive deliberation, and consensus-building. These are ideals we find everywhere in our field, most recently in op-eds that promote, as John Duffy puts it, "conditions of friendship between readers and writer," the teaching of which is posited as an antidote to the alarming enmity of our political sphere (242).

The problem is that neoliberalism strips away all of necessary preconditions that this Habermasian communicative ideal depends on. Booth himself anticipated the assault on civic space for civil discourse in a chillingly prescient footnote near the very end of *Modern Dogma*. In that footnote, he despairs that democratic institutions and commitments to mutuality will survive within an "inhumane economic system" increasingly defined by "viciousness, deception, and privatization to the point of psychosis" (201–02n32). At the moment he was completing his book for publication in 1974, the tenets of neoliberalism were just being advanced as a solution to economic crisis and slump. In fact, the University of Chicago, with its "Chicago School" followers of Milton Friedman, was one of the earliest incubators for what Booth was already beginning to recognize as a full assault on any notion of shared responsibility and public good.

So what to do? I think part of the answer is found in cultivating as much as possible the spaces of solidarity and democracy where people really can come together for genuine exchange. That means not falling into the traps of competition: my program versus theirs, tenure-track versus lecturers. Indeed, to take inspiration from the Combahee and Black Lives Matter slogans, an important slogan for academics might be "When adjunct faculty get free, we all get free." Part of the answer rests in teaching ourselves and our students critical apperception of neoliberalism's fuzzy language games as well as the material economic, political, and social reordering these games assist. From those spaces of solidarity and in response to what we discern, we can strive to practice as democratically as we can and with as many others as we can muster what Marxist linguist Jean-Jacques Lecercle names as the antidote to *la langue de coton*: that is, *la langue de bois*, or wooden language, that our rhetorical theories have largely ignored and our pedagogies have tended to counsel against. *La langue de bois*, explains Lecercle, expresses a position, it expresses opposition and who it is opposed to, and it also assembles friends and allies (217).

I know that when we think about solving problems together, the idea of *la langue de bois*—the language of resistance, opposition, and protest—may not be foremost. Few of us have had any kind of formal education in the rich tradition of social movement rhetorics. We're trained instead to try to act as rhetorically savvy individuals, each left to devise our own "Everyone should have a plan" solution for every emergency that descends on our programs. But some of you are also from campuses that have recently won important victories for your programs and students because faculty went on strike. And even if you are at a private college or in the kind of "right to work" state we may all soon find ourselves in, if you look back just a few decades, you'll likely find plenty of *la langue de bois* on your campus—the mass rhetorical action necessary to win the university access, equality, and democracy now being dismantled, a social rhetorical spirit we can defend and reclaim.

Works Cited

Booth, Wayne C. *Modern Dogma and the Rhetoric of Assent*. U of Chicago P, 1974.

Bunsis, Howard. "Financial Analysis of the University of Vermont and the Environment for Labor in the Trump Administration." UVM United Academics AFT/AAUP, Jan. 2017, Burlington, Vermont. Address.

Combahee River Collective. "Combahee River Collective Statement." *Home Girls: A Black Feminist Anthology*, edited by Barbara Smith. Kitchen Table: Women of Color P, 1983, pp. 272–82.

Duffy, John. "The Good Writer: Virtue Ethics and the Teaching of Writing." *College English*, vol. 79, no. 3, 2017, pp. 229–50.

The Economist, 6 Jan 2011, vol. 398, no. 8715.

Fury, Jerry. "Northwestern National Life." jerryfury.com/northwestern-national-life.

Frazier, Demita, Barbara Ransby, Barbara Smith, Sharon Smith, and Keeanga-Yamahtta Taylor. "How We Get Free: The 40th Anniversary of the Combahee River Collective." Socialism 2017, 7 July 2017, Chicago.

Golus, Carrie. "Which Side Are You On?: A Look Back at the Sit-In of the Administration Building of 1969." *The CORE: College Magazine of the University of Chicago*, 2010, thecore.uchicago.edu/winter2010/which-side.shtml.

Jordan, June. "Poem Towards a Final Solution." *Living Room*. Thunder's Mouth P, pp. 95–97.

Lecercle, Jean-Jacques. *A Marxist Philosophy of Language*. Translated by Gregory Elliott. Haymarket Books, 2009.
Rosowsky, David. "The Flywheel." *Across the Green*, Apr. 2016, www.uvm.edu/provost/ATG April 2016.pdf. Memo.
Sword, Helen. "The Writer's Diet Test." writersdiet.com/test.php.
Welch, Nancy. "Informed, Passionate, and Disorderly: Uncivil Rhetoric in a New Gilded Age." *Community Literacy Journal*, vol. 7, no. 1, 2012, pp. 33–51.
—. "*La Langue de Coton*: How Neoliberal Rhetoric Pulls the Wool over Shared Governance." *Pedagogy*, vol. 11, no. 3, 2011, pp. 545–53.
Welch, Nancy, and Tony Scott, editors. *Composition in the Age of Austerity*. Utah State UP, 2016.

Nancy Welch is professor of English at the University of Vermont. Her most recent scholarship, focused on public writing, neoliberal rhetoric, and social movement and working-class rhetorics, has appeared in *College English*, *College Composition and Communication*, *Community Literacy Journal*, and *Pedagogy*. Her books include *Living Room: Teaching Public Writing in a Privatized World*, *Getting Restless: Rethinking Revision in Writing Instruction*, *The Road from Prosperity: Stories*, and a forthcoming volume, *Unruly Rhetorics*, co-edited with Jonathan Alexander and Susan Jarratt. Her article "'We're Here and We're Not Going Anywhere': Why Working-Class Rhetorical Action *Still* Matters" received *College English*'s Richard C. Ohmann Outstanding Article award.

Austerity and the Scales of Writing Program Administration: Some Reflections on the 2017 CWPA Conference

Tony Scott

ABSTRACT

In July 2017, Nancy Welch and I were invited to be co-plenary speakers at the annual CWPA conference in Knoxville, Tennessee. The conference theme was "Solving Problems Together: Agency and Advocacy in an Age of Austerity." In addition to delivering plenary addresses, we were asked to deliver "fly on the wall" reflections on the sessions we attended at the Saturday luncheon. I spoke from the notes I took as I made my way through the sessions. What follows starts from those notes, but it also benefits from the time for reflection I have had since.

With the collection *Composition in the Age of Austerity* Nancy Welch and I intended to provide a political economic frame for understanding and theorizing postsecondary writing education as actually existing, everyday material practice. Chapters describe the on-the-ground effects of externally imposed assessment and curricular mandates; how budget cuts and Common Core state standards reshape community-focused and K–12 related literacy projects; and how the precarity of composition's instructorate shapes the learning environments of postsecondary writing education. The collection makes connections across these scenes and frames them within the broader economic and cultural shifts that are transforming higher education: for instance, tracking how long-term trends in state and federal budgeting and in what is considered private and public responsibility play out at particular sites with particular people. So the collection encourages readers to do composition theory through seeing composition work across scales.

As I have had the opportunity to reflect on the sessions I attended at the 2017 CWPA conference, I find myself again continually returning to questions of scale. The scales of WPA work are concurrently material and temporal ("space/time")—simultaneously grounded in singular places and moments, and extending outward to broader frontiers that are consequential yet murky. WPAs are responsible for tens, often hundreds, of sections of writing involving thousands of students each year. We are tasked with leading the development of curricula and conducting program assessments, and we are in ongoing dialogues with students, teachers, departments, colleges, and whole institutions. We use various methods and frames to track and reflect on what is happening with student learning; we fight instructional budget cuts and course cap expansions and try to forecast and adjust to their effects; we look for alignments and incongruities across stated curricular philosophies and placement assessments; and we respond to economic and institutional imperatives overwhich we often have little or no control. Because thinking and working across these space/time scales is a substantial part of what WPA's do, when we encounter important new ways of understanding aspects of composition education, we can't just consider how *we ourselves* feel about them, or stop at wondering how they might shape *our own* research and the courses we ourselves teach: we are also obliged to consider how they might influence the curricular articulations, procedural mechanisms, and pedagogies of entire programs. Though it is not often acknowledged in the scholarship, if ideas emerging within research in writing studies are to have much influence on *actually existing* pedagogical practices, they must somehow be scaled across the stressed, economically and politically troubled apparatus of contemporary writing programs.

As unwieldy as they are, the space/time scales of writing programs are made even more complex by their subsumption within accreditation organizations, state systems, and cross-institutional curricular and assessment regimes. Depending on the site, some of the most familiar forms that WPA work assumes—curricular descriptions, outcomes statements, program assessments, professional development workshops—can serve as channeling mechanisms for these varied, sometimes uneasily melded, interests. This is evident, for instance, in polyvocal materials like syllabi and outcomes statements, which can contain directly copied or patchworked bureaucratic passages with origins and intentions unknown by even the teachers using them. Because WPA work is positioned at the nexus of these various, unwieldy scales of influence, it affords a unique perspective on postsecondary writing education as actual happening but that can easily become bewildering and overwhelming. Attending sessions at the CWPA conference in Knoxville and hearing about the thoughtful, innovative things people are doing under often difficult circumstances emphasized for me the importance of focusing on how to understand more about, and gain purchase on, the ways that ideas, languages, people, and organizations relate across places and times.

On the first day of the conference, Aubrey Schiavone was presented with the 2017 Award for Graduate Writing in WPA Studies for her dissertation, *Understanding the Literacies of Working Class First-Generation College Students*. Schiavone's research highlights the unique competencies of a student population that is too often either institutionally overlooked or, when acknowledged, categorically distinguished by its perceived deficiencies. She found that the students with whom she worked in her study were particularly adept at financial literacies, rhetorical listening, invitational rhetoric, and audience awareness. Due in part to their experiences as workers outside of school, participating students had a generally more expansive understanding of writing and rhetoric than those who have had little or no work experience. Schiavone's research highlights how different literacies and the lived experiences, cultures, and identities with which they are related, can be valorized or made to seem irrelevant depending on when, where, and how they manifest. In this way, her work relates to a rich body of scalar scholarship in literacy studies, sociolinguistics, and mobility studies. Among the concerns of this research is how political and social processes shape learning environments and how language practices in one space/time connect to resources and competencies that have originated elsewhere. Scalar research also examines how individual experiences with literacy and language are translated into bureaucratic discourses, how bureaucracies use standardized mechanisms of valuation (such as assessments) to extend their authority and influence, and how particular ideas, practices, and regimes of valuation gain "weight" or authority through their uptake and recontextualization across space/time (see Blommaert; Compton-Lilly and Halverson; Collins et al., *Globalization*; Kell).

For instance, one recent scalar study by James Collins examines the effect of broad social and bureaucratic conflicts on the educational experiences of Latino migrant schoolchildren in upstate New York. Connecting macro and micro elements, Collins makes sense of particular classroom events involving migrant children through referencing regional tensions around race, immigration, and linguistic difference, and the perceptions of multilingualism and cultural identity among the children's families and the staff at the school. A study by Rebecca Lorimer Leonard uses a form of scalar analysis to examine the possibilities and limits of multilingualism as a tool for social mobility, finding that the benefits of multilingual competence are situational and uneven across contexts. Another study by Amy Stornaiuolo and Robert Jean LeBlanc offers research on how unequally distributed and ordered resources (time, space, language, technologies) shape the interactions of a group of teachers involved in international, cross-institutional collaborations. Through making connections across space/time scales, this work challenges and enhances how we research and understand the learning environments of writing education that are our primary daily concern.

The sessions I attended at the 2017 CWPA conference reveal a strong desire among our members for more of such research that enables us to understand relationships between the micro and the macro, the granular and the aggregate. I attended a number of sessions that, similar to Schiavone's dissertation, were local in their primary focus while also being concerned with scales and mobilities. In one, presenters described the implementation of a new introductory curriculum that is intended to address problems with incivility and "post-truth" public discourse through emphasizing logical argumentation and critical thinking about sourcing. Its rationale was explained in relation to our increasingly authoritarian political context; our disciplinary concerns with rhetoric, metacognition, and transfer; and the challenges of creating an introductory curriculum that is at once politically timely, appealing to cross-campus colleagues, and capable of being promoted across large numbers of sections each semester. Another interactive session examined what can happen to curricular concepts like genre and reflection as they travel from a university curriculum to high school partners in a dual enrollment program. As those of us who attended the session discussed student reflective drafts that we were asked to assess, we also shared our thoughts about reflection as a school genre and our own positionality in relation to these students' texts. This conversation evolved into a more general discussion of teacher and institutional positionality and how dual enrollment programs create vexing issues with authority, curricular purpose, and the transfer of ideas and practices across differing educational contexts and student populations. We wondered what happens to threshold concepts—for instance, to the meanings of "genre" and "reflection"—when they travel across institutions with different goals, disciplinary moorings, bureaucracies, and assessments. These conversations are vitally important to our work at a moment in which states and private institutions are looking to dual enrollment programs as a means to make further cuts in instructional costs while generating new revenue streams that require limited overhead.

Other sessions were notably more "macro" in their scope, and focused on broad data collection and analysis. These sessions concerned how the work of teachers and students in writing programs can be related to large-scale assessment and data regimes. Several sessions described efforts to do program assessments and other forms of program-wide research using support materials, services, and data from two very prominent and interrelated national initiatives: the VALUE Initiative and the National Survey of Student Engagement (NSSE), both of which are promoted by the American Association of Colleges and Universities (AACU). The VALUE initiative is managed by a "VALUE Institute," which involves various organizational partners. These sessions were timely. The institute's "Written Communication VALUE Rubric" has become widely influential and is now being used in assessments of students' work in postsecondary writing programs across the US. An overarching goal of the project is to create a national framework for reporting and cross-institutional comparison of student performances in written communication, quantitative literacy, and critical thinking. Toward that end, it aims to scale particular outcomes and an assessment regime across states and institutions and maintain a national analytic framework using locally collected "artifacts" of students' work.

In one panel Paul Anderson described the implementation of an assessment that aligns with the AACU initiative and pointed out some of the benefits of involvement, including having a resource for comparison of student performances with a robust national dataset (Paine et al). In that same panel, Darci Thoune and Anna Knutson expertly considered their own institutional research in relation to large corpuses of data, such as that made available through the NSSE, to understand everyday teaching and program processes in order to make positive changes. However, panelists and some session attendees also astutely noted some contradictions in, and concerns with, the rhetoric and aims of the AACU project. At times, it draws its language directly from the assessment scholarship in writing and composition studies, which generally emphasizes the importance of local participation and agency in assessment design and implementation. The AACU local stance, however, is substantially muddied by the other rhetoric and stated national aspirations of this dizzyingly polycentric organizational network. The VALUE initiative is aligned with Liberal Education and America's Promise (LEAP), which promotes "essential outcomes" for nationwide adoption. VALUE, like LEAP, functions as a mobile brand that connects with product lines in which institutions can enroll. The cost of basic, entry-level participation currently starts at $6,000, for which the institution is supplied with "sampling plan guidance, access to a digital platform for submitting student artifacts, selection of one learning outcome with upload of 100 artifacts, scoring of all artifacts by certified VALUE scorers, templates for local reporting, [and] nationwide benchmark reports for context and comparison" ("VALUE Institute"). The VALUE institute points out that "participating states are working with their respective campuses to fold these results into state level decision making and information about student achievement." The importance of understanding the scales of influence in writing education could not be more apparent than in this very strategic alignment of the aims of a network of national organizations with the everyday work of teachers, students, and administrators across programs and institutions. In spite of some rhetoric that seems to support local agency in curricular goals and assessment design, the AACU and its various entities are designed and marketed for their scalability. Outcomes are externally supplied by VALUE; students' writing ("student artifacts") become a part of a national VALUE corpus, and after the samples are assessed by VALUE scorers, they can compare the results with the other participating institutions across the US.

Thinking across scales, how might the VALUE initiative relate to austerity? What are we to make of economies of scale within which a student's work/text generated for a particular class can become an artifact integrated within a large-scale assessment regime that generates aggregate data for cross-institutional comparison? How are states likely to use this work/text/artifact/data? Political economy matters in such questions. Even as the broader economy has seen a recovery since the 2007–08 crisis, funding for higher education has not. According to one recent study published by the Center on Budget and Policy Priorities, ten years after the recession, public funding for higher education is $10 billion below what it was in 2007.[1] Forty-six states are now spending less per student than prior to the recession, and in twelve of these states spending continued to be cut in 2016. The need to cover costs has led to substantial increases in tuition at public institutions, which nationally has risen by 33% since 2007–08 (Mitchell, Leachman and Masterson). In addition to the tuition increases, in order to respond to austerity's latest phase, faculty positions are being cut; courses, degree programs, and entire campuses are being eliminated; and the way that we deliver writing education continues to be transformed less by scholarly debate than by economic and operational prescription. The Tax Cuts and Jobs Act of 2017 was passed during my drafting of this piece. There is a great likelihood that this legislation will lead to even more cuts in funding to higher education, which has already been disciplined and transformed by decades of austerity. Austerity is no longer a temporary response to crisis with a view toward transcending it: it is now a philosophy of governance that is intended to normalize crisis in order to permanently change public services, or eliminate them altogether. The history is now clear. Large-scale outcomes assessments are not innately bad and can be a tool among others that help local administrators and teachers make education better; however, they have been used much too often to scale centralized authority and create efficiencies that erase local efforts to, for instance, develop more inclusive curricula and innovate in response to current research—like that conducted by Schiavone. We need to continually be aware of how large-scale inititiaves that seek to scale outcomes and assessments converge with state and institutional efforts to offset the diminishing resources for education in austerity economics.

* * *

The shift in perspectives and concerns from session to session at a conference like CWPA could not be more dramatic. In one session you may be discussing work composed by a single student writer and talking about her stance in a text, how she has been positioned by the assignment, and how race, class and cultural backgrounds can affect how individual students perform a task like reflective writing. In the next session you might be looking at nationally distributed brochures and tables that depict, and invite comparison among, quantified indicators of student performance and assessments performed by paid evaluators hundreds or thousands of miles away from the students and where they did their work. At the 2017 conference, attendees who are not in tenured positions spoke out in general meetings about the diminished agency they feel over their work, the precarity of their jobs, and the fears they now have about addressing politically charged issues in their classes and on their campuses. They made it clear that the working conditions and precarious status of most of composition's teachers are entirely relevant to curricula, particularly those that are intended to respond to authoritarianism, the current racial climate, and the threats that many of our immigrant students and colleagues are now living under each day. How do we connect the deep concerns and precarity of composition's instructorate to national initiatives like VALUE? When outcomes and assessments are integrated into an established, national system of data collection and comparison in which institutions have investment, how are part-time teachers effected? Is space for the inclusion of diverse literacies and evolving and research-driven curricular and pedagogical innovations diminished? How, for instance, does Schiavone's research about the diverse competencies our students bring into schools gain influence within a professional scene that includes nationally scaled outcomes valuation like the one being promoted and administered by the VALUE institute? Because WPA work does not afford the luxuries of stopping at critique or settling for "ought to," but must continually be concerned with "how," these are the types of vital questions concerning materiality, work and scale in postsecondary writing education that the CWPA conference can bring to the fore.

As always, when I attended the sessions at last year's CWPA conference, I was impressed by the broad ranges of skills, the deep and sincere commitments to writing education, the dedicated responsiveness, and just the sheer hard work of my colleagues. The call for the 2018 CWPA conference, which will be held in Sacramento, offers the theme "What if We Tried This?," continuing this year's discussion with an emphasis on critically informed innovation and experimentation. In these particularly troubled times in higher education, those who work in writing administration have unique, valuable perspectives on how to navigate the vexed and besieged learning environments in which most writing education is actually happening. After the many engaging conversations and sessions in which I was fortunate to participate at last year's conference, I look forward to more critical explorations of the tensions and possibilities that surround our work in Sacramento in 2018.

Notes

1. Dollars adjusted for inflation.

2. See, for instance, *Transnational Writing Program Administration* (Martins); *Composition in the Age of Austerity* (Welch and Scott); *Economies of Writing: Revaluations in Rhetoric and Composition* (Horner et al.); *Contingency, Exploitation and Solidarity: Labor and Action in English Composition* (Kahn et al.); *Rewriting Composition: Terms of Exchange* (Horner); and a special issue of *College Composition and Communication* on *The Political Economies of Composition Studies* (Alexander)—all published in the last two years.

Works Cited

Alexander, Jonathan, editor. *The Political Economies of Composition Studies*, special issue of *College Composition and Communication*, vol. 68, no. 1, 2016.
Blommaert, Jan. "Sociolinguistic Scales." *Intercultural Pragmatics*, vol. 4 no. 1, 2007, pp. 1–19.
Collins, James. "Migration, Sociolinguistic Scale, and Educational Reproduction." *Anthropology and Education Quarterly*, vol. 43, no. 2, 2012, pp. 192–213.
Collins, James, Stef Slembrouck, and Mike Baynham, editors. *Globalization and Language in Contact*. Continuum, 2009.
Collins, James, Stef Slembrouck, and Mike Baynham. "Introduction: Scale, Migration and Communicative Practice." Collins et al., *Globalization*, pp. 1–16.
Compton-Lilly, Catherine, and Erica Halverson. *Time and Space in Literacy Research*. Routledge, 2014.
Horner, Bruce. *Rewriting Composition: Terms of Exchange*. Southern Illinois UP, 2016.
Horner, Bruce, Brice Nodrquist, and Susan M. Ryan, editors. *Economies of Writing: Revaluations in Rhetoric and Composition*. Utah State UP, 2017.

Kahn, Seth, William B. Lalicker, and Amy Lynch-Biniek. *Contingency, Exploitation, and Solidarity: Labor and Action in English Composition*. WAC Clearinghouse, 2017, wac.colostate.edu/books/contingency.

Kell, Catherine. "Weighing the Scales: Recontextualization as Horizontal Scaling." Collins et al., *Globalization*, pp. 252–74.

Lorimer Leonard, Rebecca. "Multilingual Writing as Rhetorical Attunement." *College English*, vol. 76, no. 3, 2014, pp. 227–47.

Martins, David S., editor. *Transnational Writing Program Administration*. Utah State UP, 2015.

Mitchell, Michael, Michael Leachman, and Kathleen Masterson. "Funding Down, Tuition Up: State Cuts to Higher Education Threaten Quality and Affordability at Public Colleges." Center on Budget and Policy Priorities, 15 Aug. 2016, cbpp.org/research/state-budget-and-tax/funding-down-tuition-up.

Paine, Chuck, Paul Anderson, Anna Knutson, and Darci Thoune. "Innovations Derived from the CWPA/National Survey of Student Engagement Study: How a Writing Program Can Use and Extend Its Methods and Constructs." CWPA Conference, 21 July 2017, U of Tennessee Conference Center, Knoxville, TN. Panel.

Schiavone, Aubrey. *Understanding the Literacies of Working Class First-Generation College Students*. 2017. U of Michigan, PhD dissertation. Deep Blue, deepblue.lib.umich.edu/bitstream/handle/2027.42/138638/aschia_1.pdf.

Stornaiuolo, Amy, and Robert Jean LeBlanc. "Scaling as a Literacy Activity: Mobility and Educational Inequality in an Age of Global Connectivity." *Research in the Teaching of English*, vol. 50, no. 3, 2016, pp. 263–87.

"The Value Institute: Learning Outcomes Assessment at its Best." Association of American Colleges and Universities, aacu.org/VALUEInstitute.

Welch, Nancy, and Tony Scott, editors. *Composition in the Age of Austerity*. Utah State UP, 2016.

Tony Scott is associate professor in the Department of Writing Studies, Rhetoric, and Composition at Syracuse University. His scholarship includes *Dangerous Writing: Understanding the Political Economy of Composition* (Utah State University Press, 2009) and the co-edited collections *Tenured Bosses and Disposable Teachers: Writing Instruction in the Managed University* (Southern Illinois University Press, 2004) and *Composition in the Age of Austerity* (Utah State University Press, 2016). In 2014, he (with co-author Lil Brannon) won the Richard Braddock Award and the CWPA Award for Outstanding Scholarship on Writing Program Administration for the article "Democracy, Struggle, and the Praxis of Assessment."

Review Essay

Beyond Satisfaction: Assessing the Goals and Impacts of Faculty Development

E. Shelley Reid

Beach, Andrea, Mary Deane Sorcinelli, Ann E. Austin, and Jaclyn K. Rivard. *Faculty Development in the Age of Evidence: Current Practices, Future Imperatives.* Stylus Publishing, 2016. 256 pages.

Condon, William, Ellen R. Iverson, Cathryn A. Manduca, Carol Rutz, and Gudrun Willett. *Faculty Development and Student Learning: Assessing the Connections.* Indiana UP, 2016. 172 pages.

Let's start with some self-assessment. Which of these statements describe the ways you assess the effectiveness of your faculty development efforts, which might typically include teaching assistant (TA) education, new faculty orientation, pedagogy seminars, workshops, reading groups, brown bag discussions, mentoring, or online repositories:

A. We count participants to track numbers served

B. We survey participants to track their satisfaction

C. We assess the increase in the knowledge/skills of participants

D. We document the change in the behaviors/practices of participants

E. We document the increase in learning of those served by participants

F. We assess changes in the teaching culture of the institution

If you're like the majority of US and Canadian faculty developers recently surveyed, you're doing pretty well using approaches like A and B, you're perhaps using less-than-optimal strategies (such as quick self-reports) in your occasional C and D assessments, and you're doing very little or none of E and F, which to be sure are "exponentially more difficult to accomplish" (Beach et al. 109). Indeed, despite our daily efforts in faculty development in this "age of evidence," as Andrea Beach, Mary Deane Sorcinelli, Ann E. Austin, and Jaclyn K. Rivard term it, you and I are likely to be giving thoughtful advice to faculty about accumulating evidence in their own assessment processes while facing significant challenges ourselves in assessing the impact of that advice. Does our faculty development work? It's hard to know. Fortunately, William Condon, Ellen Iverson, Cathryn A. Manduca, Carol Rutz, and Gudrun Willet have scaled the exponentially difficult mountain and come back with *Faculty Development and Student Learning: Assessing the Connections*, so we have some powerful indications that it does.

You might not even think of yourself, precisely, as a faculty developer: maybe you're just a regular WPA who happens to educate the TAs or run portfolio review workshops. If faculty development is just one of a myriad of responsibilities for you, then you mostly need to know that these two books exist and what their key takeaways are—the way you may keep Alice Horning's "The Definitive Article on Class Size" or Patrick Hartwell's "Grammar, Grammars, and the Teaching of Grammar" on hand for when you need to have *that conversation again* with someone at your institution, or the way you might have a copy of Diana George's *Kitchen Cooks, Plate Twirlers, and Troubadours* or Charlton et al.'s *GenAdmin* on the shelf to remind yourself that *it's not just you* but that you belong to a vibrant community of practice. If faculty development is or becomes more central to your work, then you should read and probably own both of the books reviewed here, each of which represents significant data gathering and astute analysis by researchers and scholars at the top of their game.

Takeaway #1: Our Work Works

The first major takeaway of these studies is that, with world enough and time, we can demonstrate that faculty development improves student learning (especially when we gather and track student writing). At the end of a four-year intensive "Tracer Project," Condon et al. have documented how extended, multifaceted, locally rooted faculty development improves student learning, by evaluating Washington State University's (WSU) Critical Thinking Project (CT) and Carleton College's WAC and Quantitative Inquiry, Reasoning, and Knowledge (QuIRK) projects (11). The authors draw on a model they term the "Direct Path" (28) to establish the connection between increased student learning (as alluded to in item E, above) and increased faculty learning about teaching. The Direct Path model proposes that "faculty development does indeed lead to faculty learning, which translates to changes in classroom instruction that impact student learning" (28).

The details of the study, which used both quantitative and qualitative measures and gathered data across at least four years' worth of faculty development participation at each site, are too complex to review fully here (though if you're at all interested in educational research, you'll find the study design both fascinating and inspiring). To help give a sense of the "exponential" quality of this undertaking, though, I will highlight a few key components. Tracer Project researchers assessed whether faculty learned what was intended in their faculty development workshops at Carleton by analyzing years' worth of workshop exit surveys along with interviews of 47 faculty. Researchers at both institutions seeking to measure the effects of faculty development on teaching assessed faculty assignment prompts and conducted faculty interviews (at WSU, participants included 140 high-participating and 28 low-participating faculty), and Carleton researchers also observed and evaluated faculty class sessions. Since both institutions have longstanding student portfolio requirements, student learning was measured through assessment of student writing. When WSU rubrics that revealed clear gains for WSU faculty who participated in extended faculty development—and gains for their students—turned out not to be sensitive enough to capture significant differences among Carleton faculty's assignments and among Carleton students' writing, researchers switched to a paired-comparison method for those documents (blind ranking of an intervention document against a matched control document) pioneered by Haswell that did document gains. Finally, it's important to note that the longitudinal data allowed researchers to capture how faculty learning and integration of concepts deepened and spread over time, and how student learning improved over years rather than only weeks of experience (this is all laid out in careful detail in chapter three of Condon et al.).

In principle, this remarkable study is replicable; however, it's clear that few individual WPAs or faculty developers will be able to match it for the numbers of faculty and student documents, interviews, and observations gathered and assessed; for the length of time over which effects were traced; for the rich triangulation of data across types of faculty, students, and institutions; or for the scholarly rigor with which comparative and evaluative analyses were applied. What we can do, as Beach et al. remind us, is to assess what we can within our current resources and then refer to other comprehensive studies to show the existence of causal links that we are unable to trace (114).

And fortunately we can now all cite the Tracer Project's central results with confidence:

- Faculty who participate in extended faculty development translate that learning into their course materials and approaches more often and more successfully than faculty who do not, even when a whole institution is ostensibly involved in the project of instructional improvement (Condon et al. 70, 106, 109).
- The salutary effects of extended, focused faculty development on faculty practice not only persist over time, but continue to improve for those faculty participants (who implement more advanced strategies over time) and expand in scope to reach additional students non-participant faculty to build a culture of faculty improvement (as faculty extend strategies to more of their own courses and recommend approaches to colleagues) (Condon et al. 50–51).
- Students of faculty who participate in extended faculty development perform better in tasks related to the development initiative (e.g., critical thinking at WSU, writing and quantitative analysis at Carleton) than students from faculty who do not (Condon et al. 100, 107–109).

At WSU, for instance, assignment prompts and student writing from 28 faculty with low participation in faculty development were assessed as consistently less proficient in meeting CT objectives than assignment prompts and student writing from 100 faculty who had participated at length in either workshops or portfolio assessment (Condon et al. 100). Moreover, only 3 of 50 CT faculty interviewed did not demonstrate any additional innovation or extension of the strategies they had learned (Condon et al. 51). And at Carleton, not only was student writing from high faculty development participants ranked better by faculty evaluators than student writing from other faculty (paralleling results at WSU), but the students also recognized their learning gains: "the likelihood that a student would choose a paper from a given faculty member's course" to represent his or her best writing in his or her junior portfolio "was in direct proportion to the number of faculty development events the faculty member had attended" (Condon et al. 109). The Tracer Project has demonstrated a Direct Path from extended, focused faculty development to student improvement, and confirmed the "large leveraging effect" of faculty development initiatives (50)—and those results should give all of us motivation and opportunity to seek ways to sustain and improve our faculty development efforts.

Takeaway #2: Our Workshops Need Work

A second takeaway from these studies is that successful faculty development includes—and requires—much more than workshops. The impressive results of the Tracer Project, unfortunately, do not mean that you or I can now argue that our September brown bag lunch discussion about responding to student writing will by itself have a beneficial effect on student learning. That brown bag chat is in good company, to be sure; such one-shot workshops are still pervasive in faculty development efforts across higher education, as demonstrated by Beach et al. Their study has two parts: an extended survey of 385 faculty developers in the US and Canada from a wide range of institution types, complemented by structured interviews with 120 participants who are directors of campus faculty development centers (hereafter referred to by a common catchall term, centers for teaching excellence or CTEs), both of which data sets closely parallel information gathered in their 2006 study (17; see also Sorcinelli et al.). In both parts, Beach et al. asked about current structures and practices, faculty development priorities, and future goals for faculty support. According to the surveys, short workshops remain by far the most frequently used form of faculty support offered by CTEs across all institutional types; they also topped the list of what CTE directors identified as their offices' "signature approaches" (78). Next most frequently mentioned in both the survey and the interviews are one-on-one consultations, also likely to be isolated learning events (78).

These discrete options are convenient for busy faculty and can spark further interest in pedagogical learning, yet Beach et al. find their prevalence troubling, since research demonstrates that short-form interventions are "less likely to provide the sustained support needed as instructors strive to change aspects of their work" (78; as evidence, they cite Chism et al.'s and Henderson et al.'s reviews of recent faculty development research). Perhaps recognizing such limitations, CTE directors chose not to elaborate much about their workshops or consultations during their interviews; they were much more likely to give details about faculty learning communities, discipline- or unit-based programs, and long-form institutes or retreats (81–83). Faculty learning communities also topped the list of programming directors hoped to expand (Beach et al. 85). These recognitions of the value of long-form faculty development match the recommendations articulated by Condon et al., who argue that faculty learning needs to be iterative, extended, and focused on "providing faculty with the tools to continue innovating" after the formal support concludes (120). While the lunch discussion about grading might be lively, we owe our colleagues—and we will get our best returns on investment from—the kind of high-impact learning we provide for our students: extended, problem-based, multimodal, peer-engaged, active and reflective.

We may also benefit from rethinking a centralized, direct-instruction model as the sole vector for faculty support. While CTE directors and scholars acknowledge the power of faculty development extended over time,

Beach et al.'s study shows an increase in centralization of faculty development efforts that may limit the ways that CTEs can extend faculty support across institutional boundaries. The study's authors note the political advantages of having faculty development move "from the margins toward the core of the institution" (Beach et al. 42); WPAs are certainly familiar with the benefits that can accrue from program work "coordinated by an identifiable, centralized unit with professional staff" (40). Such centralization, though, might also contribute to what Beach et al. see as an unexpectedly low incidence of CTE collaboration with other units (37).

The effects of that kind of mission isolation are particularly important to consider given the results of Condon et al.'s more context-focused inquiries. They document a crucial yet often overlooked network of faculty development opportunities that are currently camouflaged as program or unit assessment, curriculum planning and development, and unit-based initiatives—what they call "routine, non-programmed learning" (8) that can add up to an institutional culture of faculty development. These deliberate efforts to identify not just a Direct Path model for faculty development but also a richly contextualized picture of faculty learning can help us see more diverse areas for faculty development growth. Condon et al.'s signature example of this decentralized faculty development comes from faculty participation in portfolio assessment. At WSU, for instance, each of the 40 faculty interviewed about their service as raters of students' mid-career portfolios could point to significant improvements in their own assignment design that resulted directly from their assessment experience (Condon et al. 59), even though no overt efforts were made to frame the work as faculty development. These results were echoed by Carleton faculty in their interviews about portfolio rating; researchers also point to the ways in which routine activities such as promotion reviews and accreditation-focused assessments are likely contributing to a culture of faculty development at Carleton (23).

Moreover, Condon et al.'s review of this broader picture, in which faculty development is defined as "as any activity that provides faculty and staff with new ideas for teaching . . . or with tools to . . . improve their current methods" (18), offers a way to rebut the myth that faculty (especially at large universities) don't really care about improving their teaching. The researchers were pleasantly surprised, for example, that out of 148 responding faculty at WSU, only 3 reported that they had not attended a single event that they construed as supporting their learning about teaching. As a result, the researchers' comparison group had to be formed from "low participators" rather than "non-participators" (17). Even if a somewhat greater portion of faculty in the 65% who didn't choose to take the WSU survey were uninvolved in faculty development, the data still provide a strong counterpoint to the "disinterested faculty" story. Keeping this broad view helps faculty developers move forward in several ways. If we underestimate the pedagogical learning potential of a portfolio assessment or a curriculum committee, we may under-pitch our next faculty development efforts by assuming our audiences are more resistant or less informed than they really are. And I find myself wondering: if an annual program review or peer evaluation sequence is, on its own, providing support for faculty learning, what else might those faculty accomplish with even the smallest of nudges toward more deliberate, reflective consideration of pedagogical approaches?

Both sets of researchers thus argue that faculty developers should collaborate with other units and seek ways to track the "hidden" network of faculty development experiences offered in departments and programs in order to best meet faculty needs. Beach et al. identify "faculty development in disciplines" as an "emergent theme" in CTE directors' responses that should be pursued (76). A number of directors, for instance, saw unit-based assessment initiatives as an important opportunity for faculty learning. One community college leader noted the need to "Increasingly move toward program-level curriculum development support (including the assessment of program learning outcomes)—which also leads to just-in-time faculty development with all members of academic units (not just those who would otherwise come to the Centre)" (97). Similarly, a director at a comprehensive university explained that "the culture of the academy is what's/who's down the hall" and predicted an increase in faculty development designed "in a distributed model with support in the departments" (102). Beach et al. conclude, echoing Condon et al., that we need to "envision faculty development as everyone's work" drawing on "the expertise and knowledge from a range of offices" and institutional units (143–44). Together, the studies not only demonstrate that faculty development produces a strong return on investment, but call on faculty developers to look beyond the borders of the single workshop to create—and/or recognize—extended, localized, routinized opportunities that support individual faculty learning and help build a wider culture in which faculty improvement is "in the air" (Condon et al. 89) and not just at the lunch table.

Takeaway #3: Our Work Takes Work

A third takeaway is that efforts in faculty development face significant limitations, even in well-resourced institutions and programs, and require persistence and ingenuity from faculty developers. Neither of these books is inclined to blind optimism: scholars and participants alike acknowledge how difficult faculty development in postsecondary education is, how challenging the leadership and oversight of faculty learning is, and how taxing the assessment of these efforts can be. Faculty learning isn't magically any faster or more linear than student learning, and faculty even at teaching institutions like Carleton can still be surprised at the amount of ongoing pedagogical learning they can be invited to engage in (Condon et al. 83). Productive faculty development programs can be set aside when external funding dries up (as was the case with WSU's four-year FIPSE-funded CT project) or dismantled altogether (as was the case with WSU's Center for Teaching and Learning with Technology, which reorganized and then disbanded to make room for other university endeavors) (Condon et al. 21). They can also be mandated to serve primarily as support for external objectives such as directives from accrediting bodies, as a plurality of community college CTE directors worried about (Beach et al. 32). Meanwhile, CTEs face some of the same leadership and sustainability challenges that WPAs have recognized: nearly half of CTE directors are 55 or older, three-quarters of them are women, and very nearly all of them are white, suggesting that we need to pay more explicit attention to expanding pathways into the profession as a way of encouraging a more diverse and sustainable community (Beach et al. 129). There is little room here for thinking, "Well, it's all fine for *them* to recommend actions; *they've* got it easy"—and thus a lot of room for bucking up and moving forward.

Because we need to move forward. Condon et al. directly acknowledge the fundamental role that financial resources play in indicating institutional priorities for faculty development and compensating busy faculty for their time, even if we assume that large numbers of faculty truly want to improve their teaching (119). And both sets of authors point to the ways in which institutional reward structures—in hiring, promotion, and program recognition, for both tenure-line and contingent faculty—have the power to sustain or dissipate faculty efforts to improve as teachers. Those sorts of institutional changes don't happen without partnerships that can apply ongoing pressure from multiple vectors. And they don't happen without evidence.

Perhaps counterintuitively, I find myself energized by the gaps these books reveal in my own and my institution's faculty development practices. Our small CTE hasn't built many partnerships with other academic units, but it's encouraging to discover that my efforts this past year to construct faculty development programming with our school of business are not just a randomly fortuitous connection but should—according to the best research in the field—become a model for other programming. I'm not desperately seeking minions; I'm joining a national movement to foster nascent efforts in localized faculty learning in order to help sustain a university-wide culture supporting excellent teaching. (Yes, that's the ticket!) Likewise, I can now reframe the moment a decade ago when my co-researchers and I first experienced how difficult it was to measure the impact of even a full-semester composition pedagogy seminar on TAs' principles and practices, compared with the multitude of factors influencing their teaching (for a look at the graph that still gives us shivers, see Reid et al. 43). It's not just that I can better recognize some of what we were up against in light of the current research. More to the point, if I can rely on a study like Condon et al. to support my arguments about that final link (yes, good faculty development does improve student learning), I discover that I'm more willing to look for ways to build out the first half of the chain with richer assessments of what faculty take away from our programs.

Takeaway #4: We Have Our Work Cut Out for Us

Finally, these books confirm not only that WPAs often operate as crucial actors in institution-wide faculty development efforts, but should endeavor to become more visible in these roles. I have a vivid "aha!" memory of the first time I connected the work of WPAs to the work of CTE directors, after spotting Doug Hesse make the move from one office to the other and so catching a glimpse of a possible path for my own career. Yet although I continue to regularly encounter CTE directors who have come out of writing programs, I haven't seen that connection identified in more general faculty development literature. Indeed, while 42% of respondents to Beach et al.'s survey said they had collaborated with writing *centers*, and 30% said they knew of a writing center that was supporting faculty development, other writing programs remain invisible in the survey, and overall, the researchers report that respondents "did not perceive much relevant programming emerging from other units on campus" (Beach et al. 36–37). Writing programs could easily be among the stars of the unit-based collaborations that both sets of researchers value; moreover, WPAs have specific contributions to make to school-wide faculty development.

Beyond our substantial experience in actual faculty development programming, I'll note three of those possible contributions here, but I encourage you to consider other ways your resources, programming, and expertise align with what is or should be your school's effort to support extended, distributed, assessable faculty development. First, Condon et al.'s study affirms that WPAs often hold the keys to an institution's largest learning-focused dataset, in our access to and experience assessing student writing. At the most concrete level, there simply would have been no Direct Path for the Tracer Project to measure without the huge repositories of student portfolios at WSU and Carleton. (Condon et al. state directly, "If a campus does not have an archive [of student course work] already, it must start one" [43].) It would also have been difficult for the project to proceed without the expertise of composition professionals: we know better than anyone else what it takes to successfully prompt, instruct, and especially assess student writing, and the ongoing shift from assessing students' localized, declarative knowledge to measuring their thinking and reasoning capabilities across multiple disciplines nearly always means that writing will be involved.

Moreover, WPAs often come to outcomes assessment understanding it as a learning opportunity rather than only an administrative exercise, making us crucial partners in the upcoming decades. Beach et al.'s argument that our current environment is "the age of evidence" for faculty developers—an age influenced strongly by institutional, professional, and political demands for assessment of student learning—speaks to the need for campus leaders who can bridge the gap between external demands and internal motivations (Beach et al. 4–7, 12). As one research university CTE director puts it, they are "seeing a greater interest in data that can inform discussions of course/curriculum revision, and I think we need to be able to help faculty think through, collect, and analyze such data while also making sure we have good data about the impact of our own services" (Beach et al. 96). Whether we're contributing to student outcomes assessment as an end itself, as a site for faculty learning, or as a site for the assessment of faculty development efforts, composition scholars often have significant advantages to offer CTEs, since our scholarship on data-based program assessment is rich, often nuanced, and increasingly attentive to institutional assessment challenges such as racial bias, contingent faculty status, and local vs. national outcomes.

Finally, Beach et al. draw on a growing body of research positioning faculty developers generally and CTE directors specifically as "change agents" in the larger institution who hope to be "perceived as champions of the faculty [and of student learning] and not as the handmaids of the administration" (147; see also Schroeder). That sort of language resonates strongly with me, as I expect it does for other WPAs. Our professional conversations regularly focus on the challenges and opportunities we find as we advocate for institutional change. In addition, although our programs can be marginalized in terms of resources and visibility, they are often also among the few all-campus entities already in operation, connecting faculty and students from across disciplines even as other isolating forces push toward more of a siloed or even a bunker mentality. Perhaps your own professional path won't take you into a formal position in a CTE, but as a WPA you are uniquely qualified to become one of your CTE's strongest allies. If you haven't yet built strong connections with faculty development colleagues, you should; if you currently work with them on some joint projects, you should be able to use the research from these studies to demonstrate the value of additional contributions you could be making. If Beach et al. engage with this study a third time in the 2020s, I surely would like to see them report on scores of CTE directors talking about their wildly productive collaborations with their local WPAs.

In Conclusion: The Actual Reviews

A colleague and I were recently talking about the preponderance of "good news" book reviews in academic journals, and the ways in which that trope may compromise some of the integrity of the genre. Given that conversation, I've wondered if I should manufacture some point of reproach of *Faculty Development and Student Learning* so that I can convince you I'm still in possession of my critical faculties. But beyond a mild yearning for an index, I just don't have any notable critiques. The study reported herein is meticulously designed and explained, and has fault-lines or omissions only to the degree that any measure of causality in institutional learning does—challenges due to what Beach et al. refer to as "the complex and longitudinal nature of changes" in faculty behaviors (113). The book also serves as a thorough synthesis of relevant scholarship specifically on the WSU and Carleton programs and also on faculty development assessment overall.

Condon et al.'s data analysis is dense but carefully structured and not at all unreadable; moreover, their qualitative analysis of how a culture of faculty learning can develop in an institution showcases teachers as learners in ways that are compelling and even uplifting. Even their explanation of adding a new assessment strategy partway through a major project (something I'm always telling graduate students they must not do) is persuasive. Of course they needed to switch from an open rubric to the Haswellian paired-choice ranking as a response to local conditions; how could we expect to separate A-plus faculty and students from the A-plus-plus faculty and students at a highly selective college except with finely tuned assessment practices? In sum, this is a book we need: a set of credible, data-based answers to vital questions facing us all. So if you find yourself seated near me at a conference or meeting in the next few years, you'll likely see me pull the book cover up on my tablet screen and show it to yet another person I think should read it.

Faculty Development in the Age of Evidence doesn't set out such a Herculean task, and it is perhaps not so directly relevant to the daily work of

WPAs; it thus shines a little less brightly when set next to the report from the Tracer Project. In the authors' efforts to help the CTE community see itself clearly in the current moment, I found them erring on the side of comprehensive summary of their large data set when I sometimes hoped for more consideration of causality, analysis of institutional complications, or recommendations for next steps. But that response may also reflect my own status as a relative newcomer to the community: when I look at the data, I have less context to help me assimilate all the details. And I do appreciate the care with which the researchers recruited and then attended specifically to responses from a range of institution types, from high-research universities to community colleges to small liberal arts colleges, so as not to paint all the pictures of faculty development with a research-intensive brush.

In addition to their thorough documentation of who faculty developers are now and what we are doing, I'm impressed by their concluding discussions of the future prospects of the profession. Although I've been finishing this review during a week in which Scott Adams' *Dilbert* comic strip has lampooned organizational forecasting as "guessing plus math," Beach et al. move thoughtfully beyond guessing, and their analysis has implications for faculty developers and WPAs alike. Because this study replicates a study from a decade earlier, they are able to temper predictions from current participants with analysis of how past predictions have turned out. Some of those predictions were fairly accurate (the notion that assessment of student outcomes would rise in importance); some areas of concern seem to have evolved in ways better than expected (a rise in online learning has sparked a concomitant rise in discussions of online pedagogy rather than leading only to conversations about technological tools); some goals remain consistent if not moving toward full implementation as fast as we might have hoped (we're still waiting on that paradigm shift from workshops to communities of practice) (Beach et al. 90–93). Thus I find their current recommendations—for broader scope and more scholarship in faculty development, for shared responsibility and ongoing attention to questions of diversity and representation in faculty development—well grounded in evidence and worth striving towards as I consider my own pedagogy education goals. Indeed, these books both give me hope that the work we do supporting faculty, difficult as it can be to quantify, is productive in both immediate and distant contexts; they also make me glad to be part of a broad communal effort to support faculty learning across disciplines and institutions. Wherever your faculty development practices next lead you, I hope you find that the results of these studies give you satisfying context and community for your work, too.

Works Cited

Adams, Scott. "Dilbert: Forecasts Are Guessing Plus Math." 1 Dec. 2017, dilbert.com/strip/2017-12-01.

Charlton, Colin, Jonikka Charlton, Tarez Samra Graban, Kathleen J. Ryan, and Amy Ferdinandt Stolley. *GenAdmin: Theorizing WPA Identities in the Twenty-First Century*. Parlor Press, 2011.

Chism, Nancy V. M., Matthew Holley, and Cameron J. Harris. "Researching the Impact of Educational Development: Basis for Informed Practice." *To Improve the Academy*, vol. 31, edited by James E. Garcia and Laura Cruz, Wiley, 2012, pp. 129–45.

George, Diana, editor. *Kitchen Cooks, Plate Twirlers, and Troubadours: Writing Program Administrators Tell Their Stories*. Heinemann-Boynton/Cook, 1999.

Hartwell, Patrick. "Grammar, Grammars, and the Teaching of Grammar." *College English*, vol. 47, no. 2. 1985, pp. 105–27.

Haswell, Richard H. *Contrasting Ways to Appraise Improvement in a Writing Course: Paired Comparison and Holistic*. ERIC, 1988, eric.ed.gov/?id=ED294215.

Henderson, Charles, Andrea Beach, and Noah Finkelstein. "Facilitating Change in Undergraduate STEM Instructional Practices: An Analytic Review." *Journal of Research in Science Teaching*, vol. 48, no. 8, 2011, pp. 952–84.

Horning, Alice. "The Definitive Article of Class Size." *WPA: Writing Program Administration*, vol. 31, nos. 1–2, 2007, pp. 11–34.

Reid, E. Shelley, Heidi Estrem, and Marcia Belchier. "The Effects of Writing Pedagogy Education on Graduate Teaching Assistants' Approaches to Teaching Composition." *WPA: Writing Program Administration*, vol. 36, no. 1, 2012, pp. 32–73.

Schroeder, Connie M. With contributions by Phyllis Blumberg, Nancy Van Note Chism, Catherine E. Frerichs, Susan Gano-Phillips, Devorah Lieberman, Diana G. Pace, and Tamara Rosier. *Coming in from the Margins: Faculty Development's Emerging Organizational Development Role in Institutional Change*. Stylus Publishing, 2011.

Sorcinelli, Mary Dean, Ann E. Austin, Pamela L. Eddy, Andrea L. Beach. *Creating the Future of Faculty Development: Learning from the Past, Understanding the Present*. Anker Publishing, 2006.

E. Shelley Reid is associate professor of English and director for teaching excellence in the Stearns Center for Teaching and Learning at George Mason University. Her work on teacher preparation, mentoring, and writing education has appeared in *College Composition and Communication, Composition Studies, Pedagogy, WPA: Writing Program Administration*, and *Writing Spaces*.

Book Review

Learning on the Job and Learning from the Job: A Review of *The Working Lives of New Writing Center Directors*

Brandy Lyn G. Brown

Caswell, Nicole I., Jackie Grutsch McKinney, and Rebecca Jackson. *The Working Lives of New Writing Center Directors*. Utah State UP, 2016. 256 pages.

As Mark Hall adeptly chronicles in *Around the Texts of Writing Center Work: An Inquiry-Based Approach to Tutor Education*, the "Calls for further and more rigorous research are not new in the field of Writing Center Studies . . ." (8). The four decades of sources he cites certainly bolster his claim. The most recent discussions about rigorous research in writing center studies such as Babcock and Thonus as well as Driscoll and Perdue have focused on the production—or the lack thereof—of replicable, aggregable, and data-supported research with a focus on quantitative methods. However, in recent years, several texts such as Hall's have answered the call for more research using a variety of methods. Detailing the inquiry-based learning and community of practice theories behind tutor education and analyzing the resulting writing center texts like observation reports, session notes, and blogs, Hall provides directors with the tools to analyze their own tutor education programs and texts. Mackewiecz and Thompson's 2015 book *Talk about Writing: The Tutoring Strategies of Experienced Writing Center Tutors* uses discourse analysis to identify the practices of successful writing consultants, providing much needed insight into what makes a successful writing center session and, potentially, how to replicate those sessions. While much current research in writing center studies focuses on examining what happens during sessions and how best to train tutors, Nicole I. Caswell, Jackie

Grutsch McKinney, and Rebecca Jackson's volume *The Working Lives of New Writing Center Directors* turns its attention to the profession, exploring who directs the writing center and what kind of labor is involved. This book uses detailed case studies to offer a rich picture of the wide variety of position configurations for writing center directors and provides insights into the labor writing center directors perform under those working conditions. Given that it won the International Writing Center Association's 2017 Outstanding Book award, the excellent and informative work in *Working Lives* is evident.

In addition to demonstrating the potential and depth of case study research for writing center studies, Caswell et al.'s book extends the disciplinary conversation about how the work of directing a writing center is defined and identified. Categorizing the existing scholarship in the field, the authors show that it "often tries to pin down what is 'typical' about the work of directing a writing center" by conducting surveys of directors, theorizing definitions of different types of directors, and providing anecdotal and advice narratives (5). Instead Caswell et al. wanted to listen to and privilege the voices of program directors, an impulse that led them to embrace "qualitative case-study inquiry" (9). As the authors describe, although Dave Healy suggested this type of approach to further the study of writing center directors in 1995, almost none of this work has been done since, with one exception: in 2013, Anne Ellen Geller and Harry Denny published, "Of Ladybugs, Low Status, and Loving the Job," an important companion to *Working Lives*. As I will show here, both issue serious calls for writing center studies and composition to reconsider the dominant narratives about what types of position configurations are best for writing center directors.[1]

Whereas Caswell et al. follow participants, interviewing them multiple times throughout the first year of their jobs and creating detailed profiles for each, Geller and Denny record and analyze single interviews with fourteen writing center directors, who together provide a representative sample of the profession. Despite their differing methodologies and participants, these studies elicit findings that confirm one another and should provoke a critical discussion about the configuration of writing center director positions, particularly the working conditions those positions create. Though Caswell et al.'s case study and profile approach provides great detail about the various positions their participants occupy, their nine participants fall into the two categories Geller and Denny identify as "dominant models for writing center administration: administrative professionals and tenure-track faculty" (100). These categories are important, because as both sets of authors point out, within writing center studies, tenure-track writing center director positions have long been considered essential to developing a disciplinary identity for the director and for advancing the field. This narrative has shaped how positions are configured and how graduate students are prepared to work in the field. After completing their studies, though, both sets of authors identify the need to reconsider this narrative. In their individual contributions to the introduction, Grutsch McKinney describes loosening her grip on her "previously tightly held belief that tenure-track faculty positions are always better for writing center directors" (*Working Lives* 12). Caswell identifies how conducting this research challenged her "to interrogate our disciplinary narratives about preparing graduate students for the work of writing center administration" (*Working Lives* 13). Although their analysis of which new writing center directors stayed in their jobs and which left after that first year shows that tenure-track writing center directors with PhDs in composition stayed in their positions, the more nuanced information in the individual profiles demonstrates the tension the tenure-track directors faced trying to complete the different types of labor required by their positions.

From their study, Geller and Denny learn that the aspects of writing center professionals' (WCP) positions "that turn out to be the most important to their success and satisfaction are at tension with the academic cultural actions that feed disciplinary growth and could position WCPs as central agents in the discipline of English" (97). As detailed in their study, Geller and Denny find that the tenure track position that is a part of the academic culture and meant to confer status and clout to writing center professionals also "makes them feel more torn in the everyday"; directors who are academic professionals may lack academic status, but Geller and Denny report that they "seem 'happier'" (103). Of all the ways these studies confirmed one another, encouraging this reconsideration of how writing center director positions are configured is one of the most important.

Geller and Denny may have first called for this reconsideration in 2013, but it is the more detailed case study inquiry approach of *Working Lives* which allows Caswell et al. to show why, as a field, writing center studies needs to "revise the ways we think about WCPs' position configurations" (Geller and Denny 104). Caswell et al. categorize the participants' work as disciplinary, emotional, or everyday labor: disciplinary labor is "work that involves interaction with other professionals, scholarship, or research, e.g. attending academic conferences, participating in a scholarly listserv, or writing for academic venues; might be listed on a curriculum vitae"; emotional labor is "work that involves care, mentoring, or nurturing of others; work of building and sustaining relationships; work to resolve conflicts; managing our display of emotion, usually an unstated requirement of the job"; and everyday labor is "day-to-day work of [the] job (may include teaching or other roles a s well); might be listed in an annual report or in a job description" (27). For each profile, Caswell et al. include a chart where they categorize the different types of labor discussed by the director. The charts provide an effective way to show how the labor of each position is impacted by the position configuration. The long lists of emotional and daily labor performed regularly by directors is a striking contrast to the blank space and relatively small amount of disciplinary labor. If emotional and daily labor dominate writing center directors' time in this way, then perhaps readers, like the authors, should reconsider the wisdom of writing center director positions that require disciplinary labor, or attempt to define positions in ways that better reflect the actual labor performed. As the authors discuss in their conclusion, the impact of this invisible labor is rarely considered when calculating things like course release times for directors. The everyday and emotional labor involved in directing a writing center impacts directors' lives in other ways as well. Faculty status for a director can "imply that the work is discrete, with clear beginning and end dates," yet what these case studies show is that "tasks bleed from week to week, semester to semester" (193). Caswell et al.'s findings extend Geller and Denny's call to critically reconsider how writing center director positions are configured by using the specific and local stories of these case studies to make the different types of labor involved in directing a writing center visible.

In addition to the way writing center tasks refuse to begin and end in conjunction with a typical faculty appointment, the chapters focused on Allison and Joe, the two tenure-track writing center directors participating in the study, illustrate just how difficult it is to balance the everyday and emotional labor required of directors with the disciplinary labor required of their tenure-track positions. One quick glance at Allison and Joe's labor charts reveals that, even though their more stable, tenure-track faculty lines should make them "more likely to be active in disciplinary conversations," very little of their time is devoted to this type of labor (6). Tenure-track directorships are meant, in part, to enable directors to contribute to the development of the field of writing centers studies; however, the disciplinary labor listed for these directors focuses on tutor mentoring and developing, not necessarily on contributing to the field. As Allison and Joe's division of labor demonstrates, "directors labor in untenable positions or in positions where they lack necessary resources, struggle for visibility, and thus select labor that brings them recognition and satisfaction" (14). The demands of their emotional and everyday labor make disciplinary work difficult, and, when it is done, it extends the development of their local staff and center, not necessarily the profession. Geller and Denny quote one of their anonymized participants who describes this well: "There is so much

I want to do *now* that it makes it hard to prioritize that writing work over the more immediately rewarding daily collaborative work within my writing center" (116). As each of these studies show, the emotional and everyday labor is often the least visible to others, but it is also the work that is the most immediately rewarding and dominates the time and energy of directors.

For readers of this journal, how each of these studies addresses the relationship between writing program administration and writing center administration will be of particular interest. As Geller and Denny identify when establishing WCP positions with composition studies and English, "WCPs are positioned as a substrata of writing program administration" (98). Throughout their study, Geller and Denny draw attention back to how, even with tenure-track status, writing center professionals struggle to establish a disciplinary identity for themselves as WPAs have done, or to perform the disciplinary labor required to advance their field. Given their focus on new writing center directors, Caswell et al. isolate one direct factor contributing to the differing labor conditions between writing program administrators and writing center directors, and it is worth considering in full here:

> The positions our directors took were seen as appropriate for beginners; prior experience leading a writing center was not required. They were also seen as positions for which institutional capital and contextual knowledge was not helpful; some directors who were hired into their positions were outsiders. We can contrast this with writing program director positions for which experience is often required and in which a director might first work at a campus through their pretenure days, taking on the WPA position posttenure. We wonder why such a wide gulf exists between the way writing center director and WPA positions are configured. (199–200)

Though there are certainly instances when a person hired as a writing program administrator is new to the field, or at least to the campus, writing program administrative work is understood to require institutional capital and contextual knowledge in a way that writing center work is not. Reading through the case studies in *Working Lives*, however, there is hardly one in which the new director did not face a challenge rooted in that lack of institutional capital or contextual knowledge. In contradiction to the idea that directing a writing center is work that can be taken on with little or no experience, it is important to acknowledge "the first theme that emerged in the data is that the work is difficult, often untenable, even for those 'prepared' for writing center administration" (193, emphasis removed). If, however, even those prepared for this work found it difficult, then surely it is time to reconsider the idea that very little experience in administration or local contextual knowledge is required to run a writing center.

With decreasing budgets, everyone in academia is consistently asked to do more with less, then they are often rewarded for their successes with additional responsibilities. Consequently, like Caswell et al. I do not want to "invoke a picture of the writing center director as the only overworked person in education today" (193). As these two studies demonstrate, however, traditional attitudes about the types of positions beneficial for writing center directors, and writing center studies as a discipline, may contribute to the challenges writing center directors face. Grutsch McKinney notes that this book, published after her *Peripheral Visions for Writing Centers*, was an attempt to shift her focus away from grand narratives of the field to the individuals performing the work of the field; however, even as it demonstrates the power of individual stories, *The Working Lives of New Writing Center Directors* also encourages readers to question the existing grand narrative about the best working conditions for directors. Whether or not the answer is bringing attitudes about writing center administration more in line with those about writing program administration, *Working Lives* should provoke critical discussions about writing center administration.

Note

1. Each set of authors uses different terms to describe writing center administrators. I will follow the author's lead and when referring to Geller and Denny's work use writing center professionals or WCPs as they do. When referring to Caswell et al.'s work I will use writing center directors.

Works Cited

Babcock, Rebecca Day, and Terese Thonus. *Researching the Writing Center: Towards an Evidence-Based Practice*. Peter Lang, 2012.

Driscoll, Dana Lynn, and Sherry Wynn Perdue. "RAD Research as a Framework for Writing Center Inquiry: Survey and Interview Data on Writing Center Administrators' Beliefs about Research and Research Practices." *The Writing Center Journal*, vol. 34, no. 1, 2014, pp. 105–33.

Geller, Anne Ellen, and Harry Denny. "Of Ladybugs, Low Status, and Loving the Job: Writing Center Professionals Navigating Their Careers." *The Writing Center Journal*, vol. 33, no. 1, 2013, pp. 96–129.

Hall, R. Mark. *Around the Texts of Writing Center Work: An Inquiry-Based Approach to Tutor Education*. Utah State UP, 2017.

Mackiewicz, Jo, and Isabelle Thompson. *Talk About Writing: The Tutoring Strategies of Experienced Writing Center Tutors*. Taylor and Francis, 2015.

Brandy Lyn G. Brown is assistant professor of English and writing center professional at the University of North Carolina at Pembroke. She has directed writing centers since 2010 as both an academic professional and faculty member.

Book Review

Collaborating to Support Graduate Student Writers: Working beyond Disciplinary and Institutional Silos

Daveena Tauber

Simpson, Steve, Nigel A. Caplan, Michelle Cox, and Talinn Phillips, editors. *Supporting Graduate Student Writers: Research, Curriculum, and Program Design*. U of Michigan P, 2016. 320 pages.

It is rare that an edited volume provides an overview of a field, brings together scholars from multiple disciplines, and offers a range of models for programs to consider. *Supporting Graduate Student Writers* does all of these. This volume gives us perhaps the richest description we have to date of the state of graduate communications support. The book is notable in bringing together scholars working in composition, language acquisition studies, linguistics, and English for academic purposes—fields that have worked on similar issues, but which have not always communicated amongst themselves. Likewise, it brings together a variety of methodologies, including quantitative methods, which have been historically neglected, at least in the field of composition (Johanek 9). Contributors hail from a wide range of institutions as well as a handful of countries outside the US. The publication of this book and the formation in 2014 of the Consortium on Graduate Communication (CGC) by editors Michelle Cox and Nigel Caplan attest to the need for this work and the tremendous scholarly energy around it.

Part of the reason that graduate writing has been undertheorized and graduate writers underserved is that university writing programs grew up around undergraduate and especially first-year writers. As editor Steve Simpson points out, the field of composition is a relative latecomer to a discussion that has been advanced primarily by scholars in language acquisition studies, English for academic purposes, and linguistics (3–4)—though there have been calls for graduate writing instruction scattered across other fields for decades (Bloom; Caffarella and Barnett; Delyser; Golding and Mascaro; Rose and McClafferty; Torrance, Thomas, and Robinson). Though the word "writing" appears in the title, the book actually focuses on communication more broadly.

Supporting Graduate Student Writers is organized into three sections. Part 1, "Graduate Writing Support: What Do We Know? What Do We Need to Know?" gives a useful overview of the state of graduate communication instruction. The section's first two chapters work to quantify some of what we know about graduate writing and communications support. Recognizing the need for a systematic overview of the state of graduate communications support, in chapter 1 Caplan and Cox survey the membership of the fledgling CGC in 2014, asking questions about the kinds of communication support available on their campuses. They find that 81.2% of respondents report the availability of writing classes, 87.7% report tutoring services, and 72.1% report workshops, which suggests that the preponderance of universities (at least in the US) offer some kind of assistance (28). The most startling finding was the consistently lower levels of writing support for master's students. This is notable because master's degrees now constitute the majority of US graduate degrees, comprising 83% of all graduate degrees conferred in the US 2015–16 (Okahana and Zhou 3).

In chapter 2, Paul M. Rogers, Terry Myers Zawacki, and Sarah E. Baker conduct a mixed methods study to try to capture differences in the "attitudes, beliefs, and experiences" (53) of dissertation writers and advisors at a single North American research university. Their survey was completed by 343 students, and results are broken out by first language (L1) and additional language (AL) students. (For consistency, I will use "additional language," though the book's contributors use a variety of terms.) Interestingly, these groups rated the difficulty of elements of the dissertation differently, and AL students rated *all* elements of the dissertation as more difficult. Other key survey findings were that both L1 and AL students listed conversations with their advisors as the most helpful support. Overall, the interviews found faculty frustration with students' inability to conceptualize, theorize, and generate appropriate research projects, while students expressed desire for more concrete instruction and explication. This is a substantial project, and I found myself wishing for a more systematic treatment of the results of the interviews as well as an appendix listing the questions. Some questions received significant discussion while others that interested me, such as "the degree to which [advisors] think it is their responsibility to work with their advisees on their writing" (61), received short shrift. It would have been interesting to see the results consistently broken out by disciplines as well.

The third and fourth chapters in the first section deal with the important affective and identity dimension of graduate-level communications. In chapter 3, Mary Jane Curry writes about the "disciplinary enculturation and academic identity formation" (78) that she rightly argues is more consequential to disciplinary success than the distinction between L1 and AL students that so often determines the instructional resources allocated to these groups. She makes the important point that AL status is often positioned as a *de facto* deficiency—a view that elides the cognitive and perspectival benefits associated with multilingualism and multiculturalism and that assumes that "fixing" grammar will "fix" academic writing. Curry argues that we need to consider not only the many genres involved in graduate education but also the shifting subject positions of students, including the large numbers of students entering graduate study from professions outside of academia.

In chapter 4, Christine Casanave echoes Curry in asserting that successful dissertation completion is about more than executing a writing project. Recalling the high rates of doctoral attrition in the English-dominant world (40–60%), she points out that while "writing problems" are reasonably well accounted for in the literature, challenges related to advising and student life issues are less discussed (98). She raises the question of how much advisors need to know about the nonwriting factors at play in a student's progress and argues convincingly that knowing the pertinent details of a student's struggles can make it possible to find solutions, make referrals, and even advise a student to discontinue their studies.

Part 2 covers "Issues in Graduate Program and Curriculum Design." Chapter 6 by Karyn E. Mallett, Jennifer Haan, and Anna Sophia Habib and chapter 7 by Katya Fairbanks and Shamini Dias address the important work of offering meaningful communications support to multilingual students, particularly those from international backgrounds. This is a resonant issue in an era where public universities have increasingly turned to international recruitment to bolster dwindling state education allocations *and* where xenophobic immigration policy emanates from the White House. These articles point out that AL students are often offered instruction and L1 students are not under the false assumption that only the former need it. As an alternative, Mallett et al. emphasize creating ways to integrate L1/AL instruction and creating multiple ways for students to demonstrate language competence, in part by building a culture that recognizes the value of multilingualism. Looking in more detail at a specific under represented population, chapter 8 gives useful profiles of three institutions that serve majority Latinx students. In their recommendations, the chapter's authors note the importance of mentoring and individualized instruction to underserved students—needs that these programs meet through a wide variety of ways including offering online, phone, and Skype consultations.

In chapter 7, Talinn Phillips offers both a pedagogical and an "organizational culture" rationale for establishing a separate graduate writing center (168), noting that the needs of graduate writers are not identical to those of undergraduates and that graduate students are well served by extended meeting times and the ability to meet with a single tutor. Christine Jensen Sundstrom ends the section with a chapter that provides a "cautionary tale" about the demise of a writing program at the University of Kansas. I read this account with interest because I had contacted Sundstrom after the publication of her 2014 *Composition Forum* program profile to express admiration for her program's multidisciplinary approach, only to learn with dismay that the program was being shuttered. Despite strong buy-in from disciplinary faculty and demonstrated higher completion rates among program participants, the program was defunded when its administrative parent unit was divided. Sundstrom traces the many obstacles to institutionalizing support for graduate communications and concludes that embedding communications support at both the institutional and the program level may offer greater stability.

Part 3, "Program Profiles," offers portraits of five programs that illustrate the diverse ways that universities are addressing the need for graduate communications support. The opportunity to see where and how a wide variety of institutions locate communications support will make this section particularly interesting to WPAs. For instance, Jane Freeman reports that the University of Toronto provides services through its Office of English Language and Writing Support (ELWS), housed in the School of Graduate Studies, while Sue Starfield and Pamela Mort talk about the Learning Center (LC) at the University of New South Wales, which provides services to the entire university community. At Chalmers University in Sweden, profiled by Magnus Gustafsson, Andreas Eriksson, and Anna Karlsson, Communications courses are created by the Division for Language and Communication (DLC) and are then purchased by individual programs within the university. Meanwhile, James Tierney profiles the Yale English Language Program, which is housed in the Yale Center for Teaching and Learning.

The range and configuration of services in the programs profiled will also interest program administrators, who often have to make difficult decisions about where to allocate limited resources. Many of the programs profiled report using data collection to test and adjust their offerings and several offer evidence of efficacy, which seems like a prudent move in an era of budget cutting. These programs offer a wide variety of courses—from term long classes to the University of Toronto's short, "modular" courses in oral and writing skills for both L1 and AL students. The shorter structure, they note, makes it possible to offer courses more frequently and to reach more students. Many of the programs also offer workshops, boot camps, and individual consultation.

Collaboration between communications programs and disciplinary units is another important theme in this section. The ELWS at University of Toronto serves as a resource for the faculty of many disciplines as well as a locus for faculty professional development. Yale's English Language Program has created large-scale partnerships with the schools of management and law. Tierney makes the important observation that in these kinds of consulting relationships, it is important for the learning to flow in both directions. Throughout the volume contributors note that cross-campus collaborations not only serve students, but also generate buy-in and support for writing and communications, support that serves as a protective factor against administrate overhauls.

This volume presents an encouraging view of an emerging area of academic practice and scholarship and makes several important interventions—the first of which is simply creating a space for scholars from multiple disciplines to speak to their shared issues. The book also helpfully and forcefully gives the lie to the common misperception that AL learners are "problem" writers and speakers who require remedial instruction while L1 students require no instruction in academic discourse whatsoever. The book also gives compelling examples of collaboration between communications units and disciplinary units that remind us how important it is for people who support graduate communications to educate colleagues and administrators about the fact that oral and literate practices are not simply icing on the academic cake, but rather are key ingredients.

At the same time, the volume doesn't shy away from the difficulties facing the field, one of which is the challenge of occupying a space that is still stubbornly regarded as "remedial" by some faculty. Because graduate education tends to be decentralized, another significant theme is the challenge of working with and around organizational and funding silos. Additionally, programs like many of those described in the book that are characterized by having a few full-time faculty (who may or may not be tenurable) and a plethora of teaching assistants, lecturers, and adjuncts, may be vulnerable simply because they have few permanent members with have access to institutional decision making. Further, they offer a sobering reminder of how few family wage jobs await graduates in these fields. While the vexed question of academic labor lies outside the scope of this book, it should not be far from the consideration of anyone who works in, or trains graduate students to work in, these fields.

Supporting Graduate Student Writers should be on the reading list of every WPA who works in graduate education or who is looking to expand their programs to serve graduate students. The volume is useful in informing our understanding of graduate communications pedagogy and illustrating the various ways that services and courses can be configured. Also importantly, the book provides fodder for those who are trying—sometimes against significant pushback—to make the case on their own campuses that graduate students should not "always already know how to write." This is an important book in its own right and in light of the conversations that it has generated. The fact that the Consortium on Graduate Communication now convenes an annual conference and supports an active listserv that includes many WPAs ensures that *Supporting Graduate Student Writers* remains, in the best sense, a work in progress.

Works Cited

Bloom, Lynn Z. "Why Graduate Students Can't Write: Implications of Research on Writing Anxiety for Graduate Education." *JAC*, vol. 2, nos. 1–2, 1981, pp. 103–17.

Caffarella, Rosemary S., and Bruce G. Barnett. "Teaching Doctoral Students to Become Scholarly Writers: The Importance of Giving and Receiving Critiques." *Studies in Higher Education*, vol. 25, no. 1, 2000, pp. 39–52.

Delyser, Dydia. "Teaching Graduate Students to Write: A Seminar for Thesis and Dissertation Writers." *Journal of Geography in Higher Education*, vol. 27, no. 2, 2003, pp. 169–81.

Golding, Alan, and John Mascaro. "A Survey of Graduate Writing Courses." *JAC*, vol. 6, 1985–86, pp. 167–79.

Johanek, Cindy. *Composing Research: A Contextualist Paradigm for Rhetoric and Composition*. Utah State UP, 2000.

Okahana, Hironao, and Enyu Zhou. "Graduate Enrollment and Degrees: 2006 to 2016." Council of Graduate Schools, 2017, cgsnet.org/graduate-enrollment-and-degrees.

Rose, Mike, and Karen A. McClafferty. "A Call for the Teaching of Writing in Graduate Education." *Educational Researcher*, vol. 30, no. 2, 2001, pp. 27–33.

Sundstrom, Christine Jensen. "The Graduate Writing Program at the University of Kansas: An Inter-Disciplinary, Rhetorical Genre-Based Approach to Developing Professional Identities." *Composition Forum*, vol. 29, 2014, compositionforum.com/issue/29/kansas.php.

Torrance, M., G. V. Thomas, and E. J. Robinson. "The Writing Strategies of Graduate Research Students in the Social Sciences." *Higher Education*, vol. 27, no. 3, 1994, pp. 379–92.

Announcement

The **Computers and Writing Graduate Research Network (GRN)** invites proposals for its 2018 workshop, May 24, 2018, at the Computers and Writing Conference hosted by George Mason University in Fairfax, Virginia. The GRN is an all-day preconference event, open to all registered conference participants at no charge. Roundtable discussions group those with similar interests and discussion leaders who facilitate discussion and offer suggestions for developing research projects and for finding suitable venues for publication. We encourage anyone interested or involved in graduate education and scholarship—students, professors, mentors, and interested others—to participate in this important event. The GRN welcomes those pursuing work at any stage, from those just beginning to consider ideas to those whose projects are ready to pursue publication. Participants are also invited to apply for travel funding through the GRN Travel Grant Fund. Deadline for submissions is April 24, 2018. For more information or to submit a proposal, visit our website at http://www.gradresearchnetwork.org or email Janice Walker at jwalker@georgiasouthern.edu.

TEXAS STATE UNIVERSITY
MA Rhetoric & Composition

- Explore minority rhetorics, digital literacies, writing centers, writing and empathy, and more
- Work with nationally recognized faculty
- Teach writing in high schools and universities
- Develop and lead writing initiatives
- Write professionally
- Pursue the PhD in Rhetoric and Composition

"My experience in the program has been invaluable to me as a composition instructor and to my development as a PhD student." —Casie Moreland

Graduate Assistantships, Scholarships, and Financial Aid available

CONTACT: MARC@TXSTATE.EDU 512-245-7684
MARC.ENGLISH.TXSTATE.EDU

Extending an invitation to join the

Council of

Writing Program Administrators

The Council of Writing Program Administrators offers a national network of scholarship and support for leaders of college and university writing programs.

Membership benefits include the following:

- A subscription to *WPA: Writing Program Administration*, a semi-annual refereed journal
- Invitations to the annual WPA Summer Workshops and Conferences
- Invitations to submit papers for sessions that WPA sponsors at MLA and CCCC
- Participation in the WPA Research Grant Program, which distributes several awards, ranging from $1,000 to $2,000
- Invitations to the annual WPA breakfast at CCCC and the annual WPA party at MLA
- Information about the WPA Consultant-Evaluator Service

ANNUAL DUES
Graduate Students: $20
Not on Tenure Track: $20
Regular: $40
Sustaining (voluntary): $60
Library: $80

TO JOIN
Visit us online at http://wpacouncil.org/membership or send your name, address, email address, institutional affiliation, and dues to

Michael McCamley, CWPA Secretary
University of Delaware
Department of English
212 Memorial Hall
Newark, DE 19716
mccamley@udel.edu

Broadview has you covered ...

for writing on the job

Business and Professional Writing: A Basic Guide for Americans
By Paul MacRae
978-1-55481-331-5
2016 • $39.95 • 392pp

"Paul MacRae's *Business and Professional Writing* is an excellent new entry in the field of writing textbooks. MacRae clearly has years of experience teaching writing: he knows what students need, and he knows how to convey that information in an accessible, almost conversational way. This is a practical, no-nonsense approach to professional writing." — Michael Fox, Western University

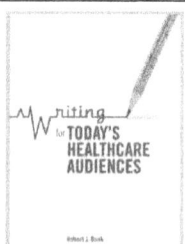

Writing for Today's Healthcare Audiences
By Robert J. Bonk
978-1-55481-149-6
2015 • $32.95 • 192pp

"Robert J. Bonk ... provides highly useful and sensible coverage of what writers need to know to craft texts within a range of healthcare professions. In concise chapters that make good use of sample documents from many medical contexts, Bonk relies on a solid rhetorical underpinning to encourage writers to be alert to the importance of purpose, audience, and genre in designing medical documents." – Stephen A. Bernhardt, University of Delaware

... and across the curriculum.

Academic Writing: Real World Topics
By Michael Rectenwald & Lisa Carl
978-1-55481-246-2
2015 • $64.95 • 720pp
Available in a Concise Edition
2016 • $39.95 • 392pp

"Rectenwald and Carl have prepared the definitive writing-across-the-curriculum textbook. This book engages students and teachers in lively and robust topics, but it also introduces them to the world of academic disciplines and their various concerns. The topics are compelling, and the concise introduction to academic writing is thorough and easily digested ... There is simply no better book that I have seen for introducing students to both college-level writing and academic discourses more generally."— Tamuira Reid, New York University

**NEW
Research Now: Contemporary Writing in the Disciplines**
Edited by Daniel Burgoyne & Richard Gooding
978-1-55481-329-2
2018 • $36.95• 400pp

Research Now: Contemporary Writing in the Disciplines gathers exciting current scholarship from across the disciplines in a concise collection of research-oriented academic prose. Most of the readings first appeared in academic journals, but there are other forms of research writing, as well, including a book chapter by a senior scholar and a proposal by a graduate student. These studies were written by researchers from around the world working in the sciences, social sciences, and humanities.

*For more information, or to order a book online, please visit www.broadviewpress.com.
If you would like to consider a text for course use, please contact examcopies@broadviewpress.com to request a complimentary examination copy.*

FENTON BOOKS
COLLEGIATE PUBLISHERS

Committed to expanding the mind-building process

When, in January 2012, we assembled the team for Fenton Books, we set two priorities: first, to provide an alternative to the small handful of large companies that now publish the commonly used college textbooks and, second, to engage students in the intellectual challenges they will encounter in college and as they develop their careers. Fenton Books also was established to promote conversation among those who seek to discuss how the publishing industry can best support the theoretical and pedagogical concerns that shape their classroom practice.

To learn more visit www.fentonbooks.com

Recently Reissued

INQUIRY, ARGUMENT, & CHANGE
A Rhetoric with Readings

BRIEF EDITION

BARBARA JO KRIEGER • PAUL G. SAINT-AMAND
WARREN A. NEAL • ALAN L. STEINBERG

"This book has several significant strengths. First, I am most impressed by the opening emphasis on writer, instead of on audience. I find Chapters 1 and 2 to both be particularly effective in introducing lots of examples of writing as a means of exploring where one already stands on a position and why, exploring gaps in one's knowledge, and exploring possibilities for filling the gaps.... Another feature I really like, which is quite different from the approach in other argument texts, is the introduction to the four general types of argumentative inquiry and then the application of the 4 questions in each of the subsequent essay assignment chapters. Students have the option to freely choose an approach for addressing the subject matter at hand. I think students will appreciate that level of freedom. On the other hand, for instructors who wish to exert a little more control, obviously one of the methods of inquiry could be selected."

—KATHLEEN HICKS, *Arizona State University*

To request an exam copy, visit:
www.fentonbooks.com

FOUNTAINHEAD PRESS

Fountainhead Press is a unique, independent publisher concerned with producing innovative, low-cost textbooks and custom products. Our mission focuses on working with universities to create ideal, program-specific texts. Importantly, we prioritize sustainable printing practices, using only FSC certified printers and printing on 30% post-consumer waste, recycled paper.

Fountainhead Press content represents the most recent conversations in teaching Composition.

Writing in Transit focuses on transfer-based learning and includes cross-disciplinary, scholarly readings.

Writing Moves constitutes a sustained inquiry into what it means to become a writer who is rhetorically aware and who can deploy a variety of strategies to compose effectively in print and digital contexts.

The Digital Writer builds upon writing that students do in their everyday lives and focuses these skills toward the kinds of texts they will create in their academic and professional careers.

Our best-selling *Praxis* offers the principles of historical rhetoric and the writing process while maintaining maximum flexibility for instructors.

Our X-Series for Professional Development offers peer-reviewed scholarly articles regarding the most pressing issues facing Composition faculty.

Four popular titles in our 12 title series

www.fountainheadpress.com

NC STATE UNIVERSITY

Master's-Level Study in Rhetoric and Composition

NC State's Master of Arts in English offers a concentration in Rhetoric and Composition that provides focused study of writing and literacies, the teaching of writing, and the role of persuasive language in academic disciplines, professional and civic life, and culture at large. The concentration offers a flexible curriculum, a nationally recognized faculty, and an award-winning GTA program.

Our M.A. program is situated in a vibrant intellectual community that also includes an M.S. degree in Technical Communication, an interdisciplinary Graduate Certificate in Digital Humanities, and an interdisciplinary Ph.D. in Communication, Rhetoric, and Digital Media. Collaboration among these programs yields a rich mix of faculty and student interests and expertise. M.A. Rhet/Comp students gain a firm theoretical foundation in both composition and rhetoric and also have opportunities to study such areas of interest as

Composition research and pedagogy I Writing and new media
Experimental and multimodal composing I Writing across the curriculum
Rhetorical history and criticism I Sociolinguistics I Professional writing
Scientific and technical communication I Writing program administration

Faculty in Writing and Rhetoric

Chris Anson I Zachary Beare I Ronisha Browdy I Helen Burgess I Michael Carter
Huiling Ding I Casie Fedukovich I Susan Katz I Hans Kellner I Ann Penrose
Stacey Pigg I David Rieder I Jason Swarts I Douglas Walls

Learn more: go.ncsu.edu/ma-rhetoric-composition
NC State. Think and Do.

M.A. COMPOSITION, RHETORIC, AND DIGITAL MEDIA

CAREERS IN:
- Teaching
- Writing
- Publishing
- Digital Media
- Research

STUDENT OPPORTUNITIES:
- Tutor in NSU's writing center
- Travel to professional conferences
- Write for NSU's literary magazine
- Work as a graduate assistant

LEARN MORE:

www.nova.edu/dwc

@nsudwc

Davie/Fort Lauderdale, Florida

PARLOR PRESS
EQUIPMENT FOR LIVING

New, in Living Color!

Type Matters: The Rhetoricity of Letterforms edited by Christopher Scott Wyatt and Dànielle Nicole DeVoss

Rhetoric and Experience Architecture edited by Liza Potts and Michael J. Salvo

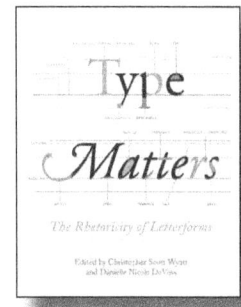

New Releases

The Framework for Success in Postsecondary Writing: Scholarship and Applications edited by Nicholas N. Behm, Sherry Rankins-Robertson, and Duane Roen

Cross-Border Networks in Writing Studies edited by Derek Mueller, Andrea Williams, Louise Wetherbee Phelps, and Jennifer Clary-Lemon

Labored: The State(ment) and Future of Work in Composition edited by Randall McClure, Dayna V. Goldstein, and Michael A. Pemberton

A Critical Look at Institutional Mission: A Guide for Writing Program Administrators edited by Joseph Janangelo

Congratulations to These Recent Award Winners!

Antiracist Writing Assessment Ecologies: Teaching and Assessing Writing for a Socially Just Future by Asao Inoue, **Best Book Award, CCCC, Best Book, Council of Writing Program Administrators (2017)**

The WPA Outcomes Statement—A Decade Later
  Edited by Nicholas N. Behm, Gregory R. Glau, Deborah H. Holdstein, Duane Roen, and Edward M. White, **Best Book Award, Council of Writing Program Adminstrators (July, 2015)**

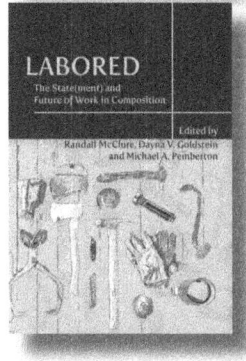

www.parlorpress.com

www.ingramcontent.com/pod-product-compliance
Lightning Source LLC
Chambersburg PA
CBHW031322160426
43196CB00007B/626